JUST another DOOR

DR SHARON ZAFFARESE-DIPPOLD

Just Another Door, © 2025 by Dr. Sharon Zaffarese-Dippold
Published by ZeeT Publishing LLC

Interior & Cover Design by www.formatting4U.com

All rights reserved. No part of this work may be used, reproduced, stored in an information retrieval system, or transmitted in any form or by any means (electronic, mechanical, photocopying, recording, or otherwise) without prior written consent by the author. Any usage of the text, except for brief quotations embodied in critical articles or reviews, without the author's permission is a violation of copyright.

Image Credits
Chapter 1—A Rescue- Dr. Dippold Designed by using Freepik AI creator. http://www.freepik.com
Chapter 2—SnowStorm- Dr. Dippold Designed by using Freepik AI creator. http://www.freepik.com
Chapter 3—Pinky Swear - Dr. Dippold Designed by using Freepik AI creator. http://www.freepik.com
Chapter 4—Marlene — Dr. Dippold Designed by using Freepik AI creator. http://www.freepik.com
Chapter 5—Teddy Bear — Dr. Dippold Designed by using Freepik AI creator. http://www.freepik.com
Chapter 6—Just Another Door https://www.shutterstock.com/g/HTWE-1962904612-
Chapter 7—Spaghetti fork - Dr. Dippold Designed by using Freepik AI creator. http://www.freepik.com
Chapter 8—Mrs. Swing- Dr. Dippold Designed by using Freepik AI creator. http://www.freepik.com
Chapter 9—The Flashlight- Dr. Dippold Designed by using Freepik AI creator. http://www.freepik.com
Chapter 10—Tree House Fort- Dr. Dippold Designed by using Freepik AI creator. http://www.freepik.com
Chapter 11—Christmas Cookies - Dr. Dippold Designed by using Freepik AI creator. http://www.freepik.com
Chapter 12—Snowflake - Dr. Dippold Designed by using Freepik AI creator. http://www.freepik.com
Chapter 13—Officer Joe- https://www.freepik.com/free-ai-image/drawings-about-legal-profession_138691823.htm
Chapter 14—Cupcake - Dr. Dippold Designed by using Freepik AI creator. http://www.freepik.com
Chapter 15—A Dream - Dr. Dippold Designed by using Freepik AI creator. http://www.freepik.com

www.GarbageBagLife.com

Dear Reader-

I am grateful that you have purchased my book, *Just Another Door*. The final book in the series is set to be released in the fall of 2026.

By sharing my deeply personal and truthful account of my experiences within the foster care system, my overarching objective as an author is to provide motivation, encouragement, and inspiration to readers, urging them to persevere in the pursuit of their aspirations and never abandon their dreams. Suicidal ideation is something I've personally grappled with as a young kid once, and looking back, I'm profoundly grateful that I didn't follow through on those destructive thoughts. Remember that you are not alone and there are people who care about you and want to help. You are not alone in the darkness.

Your future is not determined by your past.

The past does not define you; you define you, living in foster care doesn't define us. We are worth more than mere garbage bags. You're worthy of love, happiness, and all your dreams.

With deep appreciation and gratitude,
Dr. Sharon Zaffarese-Dippold

Content/Trigger Warning

This book contains graphic depictions of physical, emotional, and sexual abuse, of a child and may be disturbing and may be triggering to some readers.

If you or someone you know has experienced similar issues, please seek help from a trusted professional or helpline.

- ❖ National Suicide Hotline Number—1-800-273-8255
- ❖ SAMHSA National Helpline for Mental Health—1-800-662-HELP (4357)
- ❖ SAMHSA National Helpline for Substance Use—1-800-662-HELP (4357)
- ❖ Mental Health—211 (You can call this number for Mental Health assistance for yourself or if you are worried about someone else.
- ❖ 911—If you feel you are in a state of emergency, please call and someone to help you promptly.
- ❖ 988 Suicide Hotline—Please don't be afraid to reach out, if you have any thoughts. Someone can help you through your dark time.
- ❖ 1-888-373-7888 or text 233733 National Human Trafficking Hotline

Your future is not determined by your past.

Appreciation

Thank you, Judi Fennell (www.formatting4u.com), for your beautiful cover creation, professional guidance, support, and top-notch editing. You offer guidance for every stage involved in publishing. You are the perfect combination of everything one could hope for. I am excited for you to portray the character of Anna in the audiobooks.

Kat Sheridan, from blurbwriter.com, The book's synopsis is incredibly powerful.

Amy Mullen, I appreciate you offering your assistance in reviewing the chapters as I continue to work on them. Your long-term help is greatly appreciated.

I am grateful to my Review Team for their support and guidance throughout the writing of *Just Another Door*. Your commitment, feedback, and motivation mean a lot to me. Diane Rutkowski, Debra Holly Mosher, Melissa Wilcox, Bruce Sharpe, Gloria Thorpe, Lisa Marie Forte, Magin Clark, Melissa Lessord, Sherri Packard, Faye Cunningham.

I extend my heartfelt gratitude to my amazing family: Mark, Joseph, and Elizabeth, as well as Jessica and Forrest, whose support during this entire experience has meant the world to me and for which I am incredibly thankful. The depth of my love for all of you is immeasurable, a feeling that comes from the very core of my being.

Donation Recognition
Just Another Door
10% of all book sales

CASA
https://www.casasoutherntier.org/

CASA of Chemung County, Inc. began to form in 1988 when the New York Task Force on Permanency Planning and the Junior League of Elmira approached the Chemung County Family Court with information about the benefits to be gained through the use of CASA volunteers in family court. The first case was assigned in 1989.

In the summer of 1994, CASA received a Senate Initiative Grant from Senator Kuhl and a Schuyler County Youth Bureau grant to expand services to Schuyler County. CASA started providing services in Schuyler County in November of 1994. In 1996, a part-time supervisor was hired to cover Chemung and Schuyler Counties.

In August 2002, CASA expanded services into Steuben County, and, in January 2003, became CASA of the Southern Tier, Inc.

CASA began to serve the abused and neglected children of Yates County in November of 2021. This expansion increased the service population to over 221,000 and the coverage area to 2500 square miles.

Abused and neglected children need your voice.

CASA of the Southern Tier works to provide that voice by recruiting, training, and supporting volunteer advocates to work with children who have been abused or neglected by their primary care provider.

These volunteers work to ensure that the children they work with are able to find a safe, permanent home as quickly as possible. The best ways to support our program are to attend events, donate, and become a volunteer. Check out the buttons on the side to help today!

Information above taken from website--
https://www.casasoutherntier.org/

Storyline Details

In creating this book, the author has drawn inspiration from true events, weaving them into a captivating narrative. In order to safeguard the privacy of individuals involved, the author has made necessary alterations to names, specific locations, and certain details related to family information.

In an effort to enhance the privacy and security of the individuals featured in the story, The author has taken the liberty of creating or altering certain characters, thus adding another layer of protection.

In the fifth installment of the Garbage Bag Life series, entitled Just Another Door, the author masterfully portrays the complex language and inner thoughts of a ten-year-old child struggling to navigate the harsh realities of an abusive home environment, offering a poignant glimpse into a child's resilience and vulnerability. Given the traumatic experiences detailed by the author, Dr. Sharon Zaffarese-Dippold, this book may not be appropriate for younger readers due to its mature themes and potentially upsetting content.

It is noteworthy that the book cover does not feature an image of the child who narrates the story.

Dedications

My grandchildren

When I think of my grandchildren, my heart swells with overflowing happiness, a warmth spreading through me like sunshine, every time I see their faces.

My publishing company, known as ZeeT Publishing LLC, uses the first letter of each of my grandchildren's names in its name.

With all of my heart, MeMaw loves all of you very much!
Zeta
Elijah
Enoch
Tiberius
*(*And *Revna,* Arriving December 2025*)*

My Children
Jessica & Forrest
Joseph & Elizabeth

I owe my success to all of you; your support and guidance have been instrumental in getting me to this point. **Jessica and Joseph**, my two children, are the greatest gifts of my life, filling it with immense joy and happiness. You are such a gift to me.

My son's wife and my daughter's husband

I'm so grateful and fortunate to have two more children. Our family would not be the same without you. Your kindness, support, love, and advice are a blessing. I love you both very much.

My Brothers

Carl (Curtis)- From a young age, we were connected. Though life and foster care took us in separate directions, our hearts didn't. I'm grateful for your support in letting me share our story. I love you- Your Sister

Milton (Mick)- I'll always remember the day I found and met you as one of the best days of my life. Life took us on this journey together and I was honored to help and watch you grow. I know you are my baby brother, but you feel like one of my children. I love you -Lil' Brother.

Katherine (Kat)-A heavenly dedication to you. Despite our limited time together, we forged a bond before God called you home, allowing us to know each other a little. I think of you often- I love you Baby sister.

Although our MOTHER was unable to be a MOM and provide the care we needed, leading to our entry into the foster care system or placement with other family, we refused to let that adversity derail our ambitions of happiness and self-sufficiency. We did it. Witnessing our mother's struggles taught us valuable lessons, motivating us to ensure that we and our children had better lives.

This Book is Dedicated to US!

To My Other Biological Siblings

Life did not allow us the gratitude to know each other except for one occasion. At least we were grateful for that. Though our father was not capable of being a dad to any of us, there is still us as a result of him. We are all connected.

My Husband

I appreciate you with every book I write, and I offer each one as a heartfelt dedication. Without your unwavering support, my dream, once a distant hope, is now a tangible reality. My gratitude for all you do is immense, far beyond what a simple "thank you" can express, but it comes from a heart full of sincere appreciation.

My Heavenly Friend

Julie Schmeckenbecher- God sends Angels to help when you need them—And you were his. I wouldn't have made it through 17 years of single parenthood without you. You always helped with the kids, were my biggest fan, and always gave advice—wanted or not! And you were always right. The world won't be the same without you. **I dedicate this book to you, my heavenly friend.**

Preface

Here we go again, another car ride, another mystery door. By now, I should be used to them.

But... I'm not.

Finding a place to call home is not my dream anymore but instead, I hope I can protect myself from the people behind the door. The people who should be looking after me.

My brother Curtis is lost in another world that seems far away. Why is foster care separating us?

I used to dream of the ideal foster home—loving parents, my brother, and a horse.

At this moment, my only wish is that foster parents won't hurt me.

I can no longer dream about what I want.
I have to protect myself from what I get.

Chapter 1
A Rescue

I'm just a kid surviving in this crappy world. It shouldn't be that hard to find a nice family, but I haven't met many caring people where I've lived. What about the next one? Good or bad?

I think my case worker, Mrs. Alex, is horrible at her job because she's left me with rotten families who are not nice to kids. I don't trust her. Plus, when she leaves me with bad people, she never believes what I tell her. She thinks I'm a liar.

"How are the fries?" Mrs. Alex asks me as she jams on the brakes. "What the heck is that automobile doing?" My caseworker's screams blast through the car as she's thrown forward toward the steering wheel.

Teddy and I slam into the back of her seat and then crash to the floor. My fries fly everywhere. "What in the world, Mrs. Alex?" I shove Teddy—my brother's bear—off me, then get back on the seat. I lean ahead and look out through the windshield to check what's happening.

"Sorry, Anna. The car ahead of us stopped quickly and I think they may have hit something. It looked like a dog."

"They did *what*?" I shout in response. My brain jumps into action, moving my body without me even having to think about it, and I fling open the back door of the car.

Mrs. Alex's voice trails behind me as I run up the center of the street. My girl parts are hurting so badly because of what my old foster brother, Scott, did last night. He hurt me with his private parts. I shake my head. I'm not going to think about that right now. The pain is not going to slow me down when there's a hurt animal I hafta get to.

There's a guy bent over a—yeah, it is a dog on the road. I almost take the guy out in my hurry, but he turns at the last minute.

"Easy, kiddo. You about knocked me over."

"Why d'ya hit that dog?" My fingernails dig into my skin. I'm going to knock this guy out, no matter how old he is 'cause he hit this dog with his big truck.

The man glances up at me as he leans over the animal.

Copying him, I drop to my knees, fists clenched, ready to strike.

"Poor baby." He talks while rubbing the top of the dog's head. He wipes a tear with his free hand that slides down his cheek. Then he turns his head toward me, his gaze shifting to my clenched fists suspended in the air. "I didn't mean to hurt this dog."

The guy's crying, so I guess he means what he says.

The dog whines.

Its eyes are so big I can see all the white around them. He's afraid, I can tell. I can't be mad anymore at this man. I need to help the hurt dog.

Quick as lightning, I'm right beside the old guy, working with him to help. I slide my hand under the pup's head, the rough stones scraping against the top of my fingers. Lifting its face, I lean closer to whisper in its ear. Its fur tickles my cheek. "You're not alone. Don't be afraid. I won't leave you 'til we get you some help." Blood's dripping through my fingers and landing on the pavement.

The man moves his hands around the dog's body.

The dog growls so deep that it'd be scary except I know he's in pain.

"You aren't alone," I remind him. "I'm here with you and I'm going to help." I gently stroke the black spot on his head.

"Where did you get hurt, big boy?" The old man's gray hair is wet with sweat as he examines the rear legs.

Horns blare behind us, but we ignore the noise. In this moment, it's just us, the hurt animal, and our plans to save its life.

As I lean closer to the dog's face, he stares at me. His nostrils flare as I feel his breath on my skin. He's trying to smell me. The dog's nose, warm and damp, tickles me and sends shivers down my spine. "Poor thing. I'm sorry this happened to you. I'm here."

Time slows down as the world fades into a blur. It's just me and the dog, looking at each other. I swear I can smell the blood that's building under him and making a small puddle on the road.

"Please, mister, help him. He's hurting. I can tell." My eyes fill with tears.

"Kid, don't get too close to that dog with your face." The man nudges my shoulder.

"I need to be here and help."

"Well, the animal seems to be calm with you here. I have to find where he's wounded, so back away just a little. I don't want him to bite you because of the pain."

"Um… mister?" I take a deep breath, trying to speak despite my hoarse voice as I fight back tears. "There's, um… blood on my hands, so I think he's bleeding around its head somewhere."

The man squints as he notices my blood-stained hands. "You're right, young lady." He checks beneath the dog's head. "Luckily, it isn't a head injury, but a cut on his neck. It doesn't look too bad." He then checks the animals back again.

Glancing at my hands, I have a hard time believing that it's not a major issue. Maybe the man noticed something I can't, but when I get hurt, my cut bleeds like my leg is going to fall off and then it turns out to be nothing. Maybe it's the same for animals. I hope so.

The man pets the dog's head. "Apologies, buddy. I couldn't stop when you ran into the middle of the road. I'll get you to a vet." He looks at me. "I need to get him in my truck so I can take him to the pet doctor." The guy wraps his arms around the dog, but the pup isn't having it and bares his teeth.

"Hey, dog, this man wants to take you to a place that can make you better and save your life. He's not trying to hurt you, so please don't bite him."

The pooch continues to snarl as I rub the top of his head, but that doesn't stop the stranger from picking him up. The elderly guy doesn't seem frightened of the snarling dog.

Rubbing the fur on his head to calm it down isn't working. I decide it best to step back, giving the old man space to work.

Tightening his jaw, the man fights the dog as it wiggles everywhere. The poor animal doesn't want to be picked up, but he has to be.

The man's arm muscles pop up as he lifts the injured and scared animal. I know he's strong enough then to carry him. That makes me feel better because this is a big dog. Blood stains his white shirt.

The dog's growls and cries of pain ring in the air, as he looks afraid with his eyes bugging out. When I'm scared, I do the same thing—like yesterday in the beating room when I was alone, hoping Scott wouldn't find me.

I shiver, remembering my actual nightmare, and my girl parts throb. But I bet this dog's body hurts way worse right now. I rub its ear.

Sweat rolls down the old man's face as he carries the dog toward the vehicle.

"Anna, get away from that snarling dog! And that truck."

I don't need to turn around to know Mrs. Alex has put her two cents in. Where was she the whole time I was on the road?

"Please take care of him," I beg the man.

He nods.

"Anna, I've been standing here watching you, but now it's time to let these cars get to where they were going."

I follow Mrs. Alex back to her vehicle, heading to who-knows-where.

"Wait." Mrs. Alex pulls me back and points at my hands. "Here's a rag to wash the blood off. I'd rather you not get it all over everything."

I roll my eyes. "Yeah. That would be horrible of me," I sass back.

Mrs. Alex gives me a hankie.

"It's red."

"Yes, so?"

"Huh?" I look at her. Why did she say "so"?

"You mentioned the hankie was red. I was answering you."

"Oh." I haven't seen one of these since my first foster daddy. He would give me his hankies to clean my hands when I was done helping him in the garage or when I had a runny nose.

I miss hearing Daddy calling me Dolly.

So much has changed since then.

Just as I shut the car door, the man and the pup disappear ahead of us. I collapse, exhausted, hoping everything will be okay and that we did enough to save the poor thing. I wish someone would save *me* from my life. It's messed up how, sometimes, animals get treated better than kids in foster care.

"You did a nice thing back there, Anna. That was really kind of you." Mrs. Alex is looking at me in the review mirror.

Wow. She just gave me a compliment. Is she sick or something? "Um... thanks."

At the traffic light, she turns around. "Helping the dog came naturally to you, as if you were born to do it." She smiles. "Maybe you should think about becoming a veterinarian someday to help animals."

That's what my first daddy would tell me when I helped Mama Cat and her babies. Maybe I will. Someday.

Clutching Teddy and Raggedy in my arms, I pray.

Please, Jesus, take care of the poor dog. Help the man find a doctor. I love animals more than people. Maybe that's 'cause people hurt me, but animals never do. Mama Cat and Thunder were my best friends. Well, and you, Jesus. I hope you're still gonna be with me in this new family. I hope this one is like Momma Johnson. She protected me and looked out for me just like that stranger did for the dog. I don't think he meant to hurt the dog on purpose. I can't say that for my last foster home with the Kray's. They were mean people. Please let this family be nice, Jesus. Amen.

I glance out the window and watch the trees rush by, a sight that has become routine during these car rides. They're just reminding me I'm moving on to a new world.

I close my eyes and Momma Johnson's warm smile comes to mind, making me happy again—that is, for a moment before the rest of the world goes crazy.

I wonder how Momma Johnson is doing and if she is taking care of Patty?

Mmm. I can smell her delicious bread puddin' in my mind.

It makes me smile.

I know without a doubt that Momma Johnson is showing Patty—the doll I found in a slave tunnel—a bunch of kindness and love, just like she did with me when I was a foster kid living in her house. That is, 'til I had to move away because my birth mother, Norma, said she didn't want me to live with anyone who has a skin color different than mine.

I really hope this family is nice. Maybe they can be like that man who was nice to the dog. It's hard to find nice people in the world of foster care.

I wonder why some people become foster parents if they don't really like us.

"How are those fries?" Mrs. Alex asks.

Yeah. Her. Why did *she* ever get involved with foster care? Probably to eat the fries.

I don't giggle, but I sure want to. "Good." I hate telling her I liked them because that's what she wants, and I don't want to do anything that makes her happy since she's made my life awful. But... the fries *are* pretty amazing. Too bad they're all nasty now on the floor.

"I noticed you took your braids out. Why?"

I took them out at the beginning of the car ride and she's just noticing this now? "Um... Because I wanted to." My heart hurts at the thought. Momma Johnson gave me my braids. She took care of me. She made me beautiful. But... I'm not with her anymore, so now I'm back to messy hair and buck teeth.

Mrs. Alex doesn't ask me any more questions, but starts singing along with the radio.

I cover my ears, but that doesn't drown out her awful voice. "Um... Mrs. Alex?" I don't want to ask her this, but I can't listen to her anymore.

She stops singing. "Yes, Anna?"

"Um... Um... It's just that..." How do I say this nicely? "When you sing loud, it hurts my ears. Are you trying to sound like the singer on the radio?"

"I wish, Anna. I'm not very good, but I like to sing. It makes me feel..." She looks from the rearview mirror back to the road.

Which is probably a good thing, since she's steering the car.

After a few seconds, she glances back at me again. "Maybe you should try singing to help *you* feel better."

Feel better? Is she kidding me? I have no clue where I'm going or what is going to happen to me next, and my girl parts are still hurting like crazy, and she thinks *singing* will make my life better?

Clearly, she doesn't have a clue what it's like being a kid in foster care.

Though... my first daddy would tell me that, too. Whenever I was scared, he would encourage me to sing. And when I sing "Jesus Loves Me," I feel better—but that's because I'm singing to Jesus. But maybe they are right...

Wow. Is Mrs. Alex really trying to *help* me today for the first time in... well... ever? This is completely weird because it has always felt like she's punishing me.

With Teddy beside me, I lean back, feeling better, and shut my eyes tightly. I wish I could fall asleep right now and go somewhere else besides this new awful place.

"I gotta stop for gas. Do you want anything from the store?" Mrs. Alex pulls into a gas station in the middle of nowhere with trees all around and a small little building with a creepy man walking toward the car.

Great. Just great. "No, thanks. This isn't my new foster home, is it?" If this guy with a crooked smile and ginormous nose is my new foster father, I'm running into those woods, and no one is going to catch me.

I look around—no police cars. Perfect. No one to stop me.

Mrs. Alex turns around to look at me in the back seat. "No, Anna. I told you; we are just getting gas." She jumps as the man knocks on her window.

Slowly, she rolls it down... halfway.

Yeah, she's probably thinking the same thing that I am about this guy—he's creepy.

"Well, look at you. Hey, beautiful lady, what can I do for ya?"

"Fill it please?" Mrs. Alex uses her talking-to-the-new-foster family voice. She talks like that even when she's telling my new family bad stuff about me. But this time, there's something different. She sounds nervous as the man stares through the window at us both for a second before he heads to the gas pump.

Mrs. Alex leans over the seat. "Anna," she whispers. "Sweetie, lock your door."

I don't know what's creepier—that scary man or that Mrs. Alex called me *sweetie*.

I shrug, ignoring her like I always do—

Until the old guy presses his face against my window, smiling at me.

Ew. He doesn't have any teeth.

Okay, so maybe I *will* do as Mrs. Alex requested.

I slam the button down. The click is loud and clear.

But wait—what about the other doors?

Mrs. Alex acts like she heard my thoughts because she slides across the front seat to lock the passenger door and then turns and does the same to the back door.

Phew. Good. We are all locked in. That makes me feel better. This is like a scary movie waiting to happen at a gas station in the middle of nowhere.

Foster kid goes missing at a creepy gas station.

"You're all done," the man says. "D'ya want me to show you the bathroom, li'l lady? There's no stop for a while to use the potty." He winks at me.

I shake my head as I stare at a huge mole on his enormous nose.

"Ya sure? I don't mind showin' ya."

He keeps staring at me and I'm seriously freaked out right now. I bury my head back down into Teddy, closing my eyes to make the gas man disappear.

"We're fine, sir. If Anna had to use the bathroom, I would take her."

I open my eyes in shock. Did Mrs. Alex just stick up for me?

"'Bye, sir." She pays the guy, then rolls up her window fast.

The man doesn't budge.

"Let's get out of here, Anna."

The dust blows behind us as Mrs. Alex puts the pedal to the metal, as my first foster daddy used to say when someone peeled out of our driveway.

"Mrs. Alex?"

"Yeah, Anna?"

"That man was… strange."

"He was harmless. I think he was trying to be nice."

What is wrong with this lady? I could tell she was nervous, too, because she rolled up her window fast and sped away. Why doesn't she ever believe anything I say? Well, I don't care what she says. That was a dangerous man, and she knows it.

Exhausted, I bury my face in Teddy's fur again. I didn't sleep last night because I had to stay awake to protect myself and plan my escape out of that nasty foster home.

Now, I'm free from Scott and there's no way he could—

"Anna."

My eyes pop open. Oh, wow. I fell asleep.

"We're here."

I know that voice, though. It means that I'm at my next foster home. "I know." I also know that she now wants me to hurry and get out of the car because she has other things to do today.

What's the point of fighting against moving to all these houses anymore? I have no say, and no one cares what I think. I wish Mrs. Alex would ask me what *I* want my foster parents to be like. Why can't foster kids pick foster parents rather than the parents picking us?

Chapter 2
SnowStorm

The cooler air stings my nose a little as I stand next to the car, clutching my garbage bag in one hand, and my doll and teddy bear in the other.

Mrs. Alex points at the house, but frowns as she looks at me. "Anna, you go on up to the house and knock. I'll be there in a minute. I just spilled my briefcase all over the car seat." She grunts as she looks away from me and focuses on the mess she made.

Wouldn't *that* be terrible for her if she couldn't give the foster parents papers that say how bad I am?

As I walk toward this new world, the driveway stones crunch under my feet, leading me to another house, a world away from Momma Johnson's cozy, gingerbread-like home. This one looks scary with its black shingles—like it's hiding something.

The large flower bush in front tries to add something pretty to the house's dark look, but it's not working because there's nothing pretty about foster houses.

The enormous stone in front of me is heavy when I kick it. Rock kicking is something I like to do. I drag my garbage bag, as it scrapes across the driveway. It almost sounds like a screeching bird.

But where the heck is Mrs. Alex? I don't see her anywhere, which means I have to do this all by myself, too. Great. It makes her job easier if she doesn't have to meet the foster parents first.

I shrug. Might as well get it over with. There're many things I do myself. I can just add this to the list.

Meet foster parents alone. Check.

Just as I'm about to knock on the door, it gets flung open. A little woman with long, red hair and freckles all over her face stands there.

"Well, well. You must be Anna Snow." She reaches to grab my garbage bag from me.

With a jerk, I pull my hand back. "I'm perfectly capable of carrying my own stuff. Thanks anyway." I don't move.

For a moment, neither does this lady.

Then she reaches out for a handshake. "Look at you, using big girl words." Her smile turns to a frown.

Yep. I think she's mad. I'll have to remember this look.

Her hand floats in the air so it's even with my nose.

For a minute, I think she wants to slap my face. What does she expect me to do with that? My hands are full. I glance back up at her. "Yup. I like those big words."

"When someone holds their hand out in front of you, it means they want to shake your hand." This woman is trying to teach me something.

Well, she's not. "Yes, I know that already. My first foster daddy taught me how to shake."

She squints at me.

I can't tell if she's mad or confused; I don't know her that well. No matter what, I'm not a fan.

I heft the bags. "But as you can see, my hands are full. Plus, I don't like people to touch me."

She cocks her head, then nods. "Okay, then. Well, don't just stand there. Come in."

I look over my shoulder but still don't see Mrs. Alex. *Come on, Mrs. Alex. I don't want to go in by myself.* "I'd like to wait for my caseworker. She should be here soon."

"Now, there's no need to stand here letting the bugs in. When she gets to the house, she'll knock. Come on." She waves me in, smiling, though she sounds mean.

"Is she here? Is she here?" a little girl yells from upstairs.

"Yep, she is. Get down here so you two can meet."

Someone—I guess the little girl—stomps and bangs down the stairs. These steps are behind a wall. They're different from the ones at my old foster home with Jessica. There, Curtis and I would slide down that banister like we were sled-riding. I smile for a second; me and Curtis always had fun sledding.

I miss my brother. They took him from me at Jessica's house. He likes to hurt animals, so they said we couldn't live together anymore. What do they know? I needed him. Thinking of him still makes me sad.

A loud *crack* makes me jump.

"Darn it, Jenna! Are you okay?" the lady yells.

"Yeah, I just fell on my bum." The little girl giggles from the stairwell.

"Be careful and take your time. We don't need an ER visit."

A young girl with long, blonde hair comes running through the door, then wraps her arms around me.

I step back as she squeezes Teddy, Raggedy, and me at the same time.

The woman puts her hand on the little girl to pull her away from me. "Leave her alone, Jenna. Let her get into the house before you maul her."

Thankfully, Jenna does as she's told and let's go.

Now, I can breathe again.

"I'm so happy you're here. I'm a foster kid, too. I live here—"

"Enough, Jenna. You're overwhelming the new girl. Make yourself useful and show her to her room."

"Okay, Momma Jane. I can do that." She sing-talks to the lady.

Momma Jane? Is she going to want me to call her that? I'm not going to. There's only one Momma who'll ever be in my mind, and that's Momma Johnson.

"Are *you* my new foster mother?" I ask her.

The woman tilts her head. "Of course. Who else did you think I was?" She smiles... but it's not a friendly one.

How the heck should I know who she is? It's not like she told me. She could have introduced herself to be nice instead of leaving me to figure it out. Momma Johnson always said to be polite and introduce yourself to strangers.

"It's nice to meet you, Jane. I'm Anna Snow." Dropping my bag and friends on the floor next to my feet, I stand as straight as I can.

"Don't call me Jane. I'm Momma Jane."

I guess that answers my question. This is going to be a fight because I won't call her Momma.

"Um. Ja—"

"Come on, new girl!" Jenna says. "I can show you, our bedroom. We get to sleep in bunk beds."

I freeze. "Bu… bunk beds?"

Jane puts her hands on her hips and glares at me. "Is that a problem?"

"Uh. No. I haven't slept in a bunk bed in a long time, is all. Not since my brother, anyway." My voice cracks.

Jane sighs. "Then it's something you're used to, so you won't be scared. I have you sleeping on the top bunk, since Jenna's already claimed the bottom bed. Plus she's smaller than you."

That's how it was with my brother and me in my first foster home. He was too small for the top. A lot of bad things happened to me in that home with the foster brothers. I hope this house won't be like that one.

Someone knocks. Jane turns away from me to check it out. Good, her stares were making me uncomfortable anyway.

The door opens and Mrs. Alex finally walks in. "Hello, Jane."

"Welcome, Mrs. Alex. Did you find the place okay?" She shakes my caseworker's hand.

"Sure did. Thank you for the great directions. I see you met Anna Snow."

"Yes, we did. Jenna Storm's about to take her upstairs to get her settled into her new space so you and I can talk."

"Jenna, your last name is Storm? Mine is Snow. Put it together and we make SnowStorm." We both giggle.

"Sounds good, Mrs. Tart." Mrs. Alex just watches us.

I thought that was funny. *SnowStorm now live together.*

"Please, call us Jane and Roger."

I watch them disappear through another door.

This house is kinda weird looking on the inside. There's the doorway to go upstairs, another that goes someplace else, and the one Mrs. Alex just walked through. It's like each doorway goes to some secret location.

I shrug. Another place I have to learn.

"Come on, Anna Snow. I can't wait to show you our room." Jenna skips up the stairs.

Just Another Door

"Okay, Jenna Storm." We giggle together again.

I follow behind with my bag hitting the steps. *Clunk. Clunk. Clunk.*

Jenna stops in mid-flight, spinning around to face me. "Do you want me to carry your Teddy bear for you?"

"Nope. I'm good."

"Okay." She turns back around.

We pass two bedrooms and a bathroom on the way to...

Oh no. It's pink. All of it. And... there's a ginormous canopy bed, which, even though it's pink, is the most beautiful bed I've ever seen. This room is all fancy, and there's even a television in here. There's also a shelf full of long, skinny dolls wearing all kinds of different clothes.

Jenna nudges me out of my pink trance. "This isn't our room. Don't go in there unless Marlene invites you—and I doubt that'll happen. She's mean." Jenna shrugs. "Come on. This way."

She leads me to another room. This one is purple. It has three windows, a dresser, and... the bunkbed.

"Do you like it? Isn't it pretty?" Jenna talks loudly as she jumps onto the bottom bunk. She then points under the bed. "You can put your bag under there 'til you get unpacked. If you leave it lying around, Jane will get mad and throw your stuff away."

Jenna looks down at her lap and fidgets with her hands. For a second, I see Curtis because that's what he used to do when he was scared.

"That happened to me. Momma Jane told me to take care of my stuff, and I forgot. The next morning, my garbage bag was gone. When I asked her where it went, she told me she threw it away because I didn't take care of it like she asked me to." Jenna takes a big breath, then jumps off the bed to kneel next to it. She pulls out a bag from under it. "Luckily, Momma Jane didn't get my second garbage bag because I slid this one under the bed." She points to the space under her mattress. "So, make sure to put yours under here before we go to sleep, so you don't lose your stuff, okay?"

How awful for Jenna. My new foster mother sounds like a witch. Why would she be so mean to throw our stuff away? Some foster parents have something they do *just* to be mean to me. Mother used to put my hands under hot water. Mrs. Dorsey just plain punched me in the face. And the last home, she had a scary room where she would take kids and hurt them. "Um. Okay, but can I ask you something? Does Jane have a beating room here?"

Jenna tilts her head and scrunches her face at the same time. "A beating room? That sounds scary."

"It was, and they had one at my last foster home. The room was filled with all different kinds of belts all over the walls. She used to hit us with them."

"Wow. That's so bad. We don't have one here, but…" Jenna takes a big breath. "Stay away from the foster father." Jenna sits on the bed as I slide my garbage bag under it.

"Why? What does he do?" I sit next to her as I think about Derek and Scott. I hope this guy isn't gonna be like them.

"All I can say is to stay away from him. We need to stick together. That's what the last foster girl and I tried to do. That is, 'til he got her alone. I don't know what happened, but she left the next day." Jenna squeezes my hand.

I squeeze back. "Deal, we will try to stay together. Now, tell me about the other kids who live here besides Marlene. You already told me about her."

Though Jenna is trying to tell me about our foster brother, Barry, all I can think about is how scared Jenna acted when she was talking about my new foster father. Wonderful. My girl parts still hurt from what Scott did to it last night and now I'm scared that I could live with a grown-up Scott. Great, just great. My stomach hurts like I'm getting punched.

I watch Jenna as she keeps talking, but I can't understand anything she's saying because my mind is racing with ideas about how to protect myself here. I'll have to find a hiding place for sure. By the sounds of it, a hiding place might be an idea for Jenna, too.

Mrs. Alex's voice flies up the stairs. "Anna, can you come down here so I can see you before I need to leave?"

Already Mrs. Alex is leaving? Her time dropping me off is getting shorter and shorter. I hate her green monster car, but, at this moment, my stomach is telling me I'd rather be in her back seat, heading to some place different, than be here with a scary foster father.

Jenna stands to follow me out of the room. Just as I reach the top of the steps, she grabs my arm and pulls me close to her. "One last thing, Anna. Never pick the flowers out front. That's one mistake I made and will never do again." Jenna rubs her face.

Just as I'm about to ask her what happened, Mrs. Alex calls for me again. But I have to know. "What did she do?"

"I'll tell you about the basement later. You have to go. Your caseworker is calling."

"Come down here, please, so I can see you before I go."

What does Jenna mean about the basement? I'll make sure to ask her about it again later.

The stairs creak, sending chills down my spine. The musty smell of old wood makes me feel like I'm heading into a dungeon. My legs shake, causing my heart to race like it did when I used to race Curtis. Is my body tryin' to tell me this place isn't a good one? It sure feels that way.

What the heck's going to happen to me here?

Mrs. Alex seems to be the only person in my life that stays the same. Not that I like her, but at least she hasn't left me yet. The only thing is, I won't meet with her again until it's time for me to move.

Breathe, Anna. The only thing you can do is find a hiding place as fast as you can. You can *protect yourself.*

Mrs. Alex puts her hand on my head. "Be good here and listen to your foster parents. We don't want a repeat of what happened at the last home." She stares at me. "We don't need any stories coming up about this place."

"Stories?" Jane's voice cracks.

Mother. My first foster mother. That's who Jane sounds like with her rough voice. That mother was super wicked like the witch in OZ. I try not to shake at that memory, but… I can't.

"We definitely don't want any stories made up about our family. We are here to help kids who don't have parents." Jane's stern face glares at me.

I cross my arms. "I don't make up stories." I glare at Mrs. Alex. "I've never made up a story. Everything I've told you is real, but you don't believe me."

No one says anything, so I turn around and stomp off toward my room.

"Hold it, young lady." Jane means business. "I didn't excuse you."

I look at Jane. "What the heck does that mean?" I cross my arms again.

"In this house, you will ask to be excused from the dining table and from conversations. You will *not* just walk away from us."

Arms crossed, I stare at her. Then… I take another step in the opposite direction of my new foster mother.

"Stop!" Mrs. Alex grabs my arm. "Anna, please listen to Jane. We are running out of families that'll take you. You have to be good and follow directions."

She… She… is running out of families that want me?

Dr. Sharon Zaffarese-Dippold

Mrs. Alex just stabbed me with a knife with those words. I always thought that no one wanted me, and, now, Mrs. Alex just told me that what I've been thinking *is* right.
No one wants me.

Chapter 3
Pinky Swear

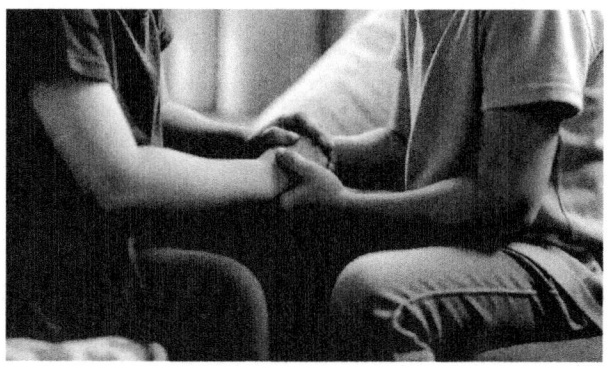

Mrs. Alex pats my head as she opens the door to leave.

It slams behind her when she does.

I stand there, frozen, as I stare after her. I can't feel my fingers or toes. The only noise I hear at the moment is chirping birds outside.

Same as always: lost and alone among strangers in a weird place. This life sucks.

I hate that I'm a foster kid. I hate that no one wants me. I hate that they think I'm garbage.

I cross my arms and squeeze. My heart pounds as I see that Jane and Jenna are watching me. What are they thinking? What are they looking for me to do? But why should *I* be the one to do anything? This isn't *my* home.

Jane sighs. "You both might as well get into the kitchen to get something to eat since it's breakfast time."

"Let's go, Anna!" Jenna grabs my hand and pulls me through a doorway that leads into the kitchen. A massive wooden table fills the whole room. I count ten chairs sitting around it.

"Jane?" I pause.

She looks at me from the refrigerator.

"Do ten people live here because there are ten chairs?"

Jane closes the fridge door. "Not right now. Only six people live here at the moment. We have that many chairs in case we get emergency foster kids."

"*Emergency* foster kids? What are those?"

Jane hands me a glass of orange juice. "Those are kids who might need a place to stay for a night or two, but not long-term."

I take a sip of my juice. "Then I guess that makes me an emergency foster kid, since I'm not planning on sticking around." I still get the creeps thinking about Jenna's warning about our foster dad.

"Well, then, Anna, you can stay here as long as you need. But since we don't have a move date set for you yet, you're not *technically* considered an emergency placement. Why don't you take a seat with that juice?"

"So how do I get one set up?"

"You can't get your own move date, Anna. The caseworker will tell us when it is. It's not your choice to leave a foster home. You're a kid, so you have no say."

Well, Jane doesn't know much, then, because I definitely had a say in the last foster home. I made sure that I was gonna leave that house, and I did.

Jane sits across from me, sipping her coffee. "You've got some serious raccoon eyes going on. Are you tired?"

She's right. I'm exhausted since I didn't get much sleep while hiding out in the beating room. "I didn't get any sleep last night." I won't tell this stranger what Scott did to me because she'll just say I'm making up stories about that family, just like Mrs. Alex says I do.

Jane huffs. "Bedtime is seven pm in this house, so, you should get plenty of sleep tonight." She heads back to the stove.

Ugh. Seven o'clock? I'll never be able to fall asleep that early.

"How old are you, Anna Snow?" Jenna asks.

Why do people like to use my first and last name together?

"I'm nine years old." Jenna smiles and I notice her front teeth stick out a little further than the others. Do kids pick on her like they do me?

"I'm ten." I crunch my corn flakes. This breakfast isn't as yummy as Momma Johnson's eggs, pancakes, and sausages, but it's better than Mrs. Dorsey's nothing. I wonder how much food I'll get here.

"Not yet, you aren't," says Jane. "You're the same age as Jenna."

Just Another Door

I look at her. "Um… You're wrong, Jane. I turned ten and yesterday was my birthday, September 19th." I take another bite of my corn flakes.

"Anna, I have plenty of other things to do today than debate you about your age and your birthday. You turn ten in a few months, but not yet."

"So, when *is* my birthday, then?" If she knows something, I want to know. After all, I only have my birthday because my teacher declared it after I'd told her I don't know when my real birthday is.

"It doesn't matter right now. And stop calling me Jane. I already told you to call me Momma Jane."

"I will not call you *Momma*." Rising from the table, I get ready for a quick exit. "I want to know when my birthday is if it's not September 19th." Don't I deserve to know this information? Other kids know when their birthday is; why can't I?

Jane walks toward me. "Let's get a few things straight, Anna. In my house, you *will* ask to be excused from the table. You do *not* just stand up and leave when you feel like it. And you *will* call me Momma Jane."

"No, I won't."

Jane shakes a finger at me. "If you think you can talk to me like that…" She puts her hands on her hips. "You can head upstairs and take a nap until you're in a better frame of mind."

My anger heats my ears like a torch in my old daddy's garage. I cross my arms. I need to move. If Jane steps closer, she'll pin me against the table. That's not good when I have to pee.

I quickly turn and head out of the room, through the entryway, and up the stairs to my new purple bedroom.

"Make sure you take care of your things. I'll get rid of anything I find lying on the floor!"

The echo of her voice follows me. Where the heck is the bathroom? I'd passed the bedrooms earlier, but hadn't seen a bathroom.

Grimacing, I clamp my knees together to prevent myself from wetting my pants. I walk past the pale pink room, then a boy's room with typical toys and cartoon posters, and, finally, a room with a gigantic bed and dresser. A picture on the nightstand of the foster parents tells me this must be where they sleep.

My stomach is like a fist punching my bladder. I can't wait another second. Thankfully, I find the bathroom at the end of the hall after glancing in the other rooms. I get in, then turn a small switch on the old-fashioned lock—and notice there's an opening in it. I stoop to check if anyone can look through it.

They can. Great! Why can I *never* feel safe in a bathroom?

I snatch a thin towel from a rack and drape it over the lock, making sure it covers the opening. Now, I can pee.

I don't have a good feeling about this place, and I'm not sure how Jane's going to act toward me. She looks like she gets mad easily, but Jenna said nothing bad about her, only the foster dad. Which is one more reason not to stay here any longer than I have to.

After washing my hands, I head past the stairs, the pink room, and then into our purple bedroom. I pull Teddy and Raggedy out from under the bed and throw them onto the top bunk.

I lay my head on Raggedy. *Hey, Raggedy. This is my new home. What do you think? I'm in a bunk bed now. I haven't been in one of these since... since... my brother Curtis.*

I bury my face into her dress. A surprise tear slides down my cheek. I swipe it away. This bed reminds me of Daddy and Curtis. This is what we slept in when we lived with Daddy. It seems like it's been forever since I lived with either of them. Do they still think about me? Does Momma Johnson? Does Jessica? Does Thunder? I wonder what Curtis is doing. I hope he's not moving as much as I am. My first daddy told me I was nine years old. Did he lie to me? Because if I was nine then, when I lived with him, I'd be ten years old now. I squeeze Raggedy as her big black eyes catch my tears. I whisper low enough so only she can hear. I have to find out how old I am. Why won't someone tell me?

My old teacher had surprised me with a birthday party, complete with colorful decorations and delicious treats. Can it be true that I am only nine years old? Absolutely not! That's out of the question. But... Janes says that I'll turn ten in a few months. Is that December? Is that January? *When is it?* I yell in my head.

What does it matter, Raggedy? No one cares anyway. It's like I'm invisible in this big world. I squeeze her harder, closing my eyes and letting my tears fall. She hides them for me in her clothing and cloth skin.

Hello, Jesus. I'm at my new home, but I'm not sure I like it here. Jenna seems nice, but I haven't met the other kids yet, and Jenna says that a girl named Marlene is mean. And Jane... I'm not sure about her either. So far, I don't like her. I definitely wouldn't want her as my mother. I know foster families are telling Mrs. Alex that they don't want me, but I hope you do. Why does my life have to be so hard? Maybe it'd be easier if I wasn't here anymore.

I wipe the tear away that slides down my face. *Do I have to die to be with you? Maybe... Maybe that would be better than where I am now, Jesus. It's sad when no one loves you or wants you, like Mrs. Alex says.*

Well, I will start looking for some hiding places tomorrow. If you have any good ideas, please let me know. Of course, I'm not sure how you would do that. Maybe someday you will talk to me. Maybe...

I yawn big, the lack of sleep catching up to me. I close my eyes.

I'm going to go. I yawn a few times. *And, Jesus? Please protect me from the foster father. According to Jenna, he's scary. Thank you for listening to me always, Anna.*

I roll over and grab Teddy, so he is on one side of me and Raggedy is on the other. I look up at the ceiling. It's right above me—so close I can put my hands flat on it, just like I used to do at Daddy's house. I'll have to be careful in the morning when I sit up, so I don't bump my head.

Tonight, when we go to bed, that's when I'll ask Jenna about the foster father. She said to stay away from him, but she didn't tell me why. But, for now, I can't keep my eyes open anymore.

The wind blows as the leaves fly by. I see Thunder standing under the pretty tree.

"Hello, Thunder, I missed you. It's been a long time since I've seen you. Are you being nice to Old Man Mike?"

The wind howls, forcing me to grip my hair to keep it from hitting me in the eyes. The cold air burns my cheeks.

As I walk toward Thunder, he turns and runs.

"Don't run! Wait for me so I can get on your back and run away with you!"

I'm running—I think—but my feet won't move.

"Wait, Thunder! Wait! Come back!"

The wind grows stronger and stronger as it streaks past my face.

"Anna, wake up. You're dreaming." A man is talking to me in a kind voice.

He sounds like Daddy—or maybe Jesus. 'Course, I'm not sure what Jesus sounds like, so maybe—

"Anna, wake up!"

My eyes jolt open, and I shriek and jerk back toward the wall when I see a man standing next to my bed.

"Well, hi there, young lady! I'm Daddy Roger, your foster father. Did you find your way around the house okay?" He stares at me.

I don't like how he's watching me, so I nod. Maybe he'll go away now.

He winks—so I guess that's a *no* about him going away. "All the girls living here know I have a secret stash of chocolate bars just for them." He looks seriously creepy—like a clown with a bald head and weird sideburns.

"I don't like chocolate." I make sure my voice sounds stern and not shaky, like the rest of my body is feeling right now. I want him to know I won't believe his attempts at being nice. Jenna warned me about him; I need to find out what she knows.

He clears his throat. "Oh. Okay." He puts his hands in his overalls. "As we get to know each other, I'll figure out what you like."

"You don't have to do that. I don't like anything." My back's firmly against Teddy and the wall, and I'm keeping my eyes on him because I'm gonna make sure he doesn't do anything to me. Jenna warned—

"Anna Snow, where are you?" Jenna—thank goodness! —walks into the bedroom. But she freezes when she sees this guy standing there.

"Well, hello, my pretty little girl. Did you meet Anna Snow already?"

Jenna looks at her feet. "Yes, Daddy Roger, I did." She wrings her hands together.

He pats her hair like people pat dogs' heads. "Good. I expect you to tell her how things work and what we like to do to have fun together."

Jenna's hands are shaking; I can see it from here. "There's no need for Jenna to do that. I don't like to have fun." I move to the edge of the bed. I'm gonna show him that I'm not afraid of him.

"Well, look at you, all sassy." His smile goes sideways on his face.

"Yep. That's what my caseworker tells me." I sit up straight so I don't slouch.

He stops petting Jenna's hair. "Would you like me to brush your hair at night? I like to do this for all the girls who live here." He smirks and winks at the same time.

Yuck. This man is gross. "I won't ever let you touch me," I snap.

He turns to leave, then stops to face me. "We'll see about that."

"No, we won't." My voice is louder than I planned.

Finally, Jenna and I are alone. He… reminds me of Derek, my old foster brother, who hurt me when he'd give me a bath. I can't shake that feeling. Roger is *not* a good man.

Jenna takes a deep breath, then runs to the bottom bunk.

I climb down. "Are you okay?"

Jenna shakes her head. "I'm okay, but I don't like him. He liked to get other girls who lived here alone and called them his favorites, but none of them would tell me what they did together. He never really talked to me much until Sally left last week, and now he says that *I'm* his favorite and that he wants to be my daddy." She grabs the pillow from her bed and hugs it.

That's exactly what I want to do with my stuffed friends when I want to keep from crying. "Has he done anything to hurt you?"

"Nope. Nothing. He's just ignored me. But he didn't ignore the other foster girls who lived here."

"Who were they? You mentioned Sally. Were there more girls?"

"Sally and Cassie lived here together for a little while. They were thirteen years old. They did everything together. They even went into the bathroom at the same time when one of them had to use the toilet or take a bath. That is… until Roger would make one of them leave. He said girls don't need to be in the bathroom with other girls."

This isn't good. Roger is just like Derek. I knew it. The way that he looked at me in the top bunk is the same way Derek would.

"Let's stay together, Anna Snow, just like Sally and Cassie did. I don't like Daddy Roger. He asked me last week if I needed any help going to the bathroom. He's never done that before."

Now I know why Jenna warned me about Roger. He's trying to get her alone in the bathroom and he might do the same to me. "Jenna, this is an important question, so I need you to tell the truth." I take a deep breath. I really don't want to know the answer to this but… I hafta. "Has he ever done anything to you?"

"No, never." She looks away from me.

"Not even in a fun way, like tickling?"

"No, he's never even hugged me. But he *would* hug Cassie and Sally before they went to bed. I just thought he liked them more than me. They didn't want to hug him, but Momma Jane made them when Daddy Roger asked for hugs."

I shiver. "Eewww, that's gross."

She giggles a little at my words, then she looks down at the ground.

"What's the matter? You seem sad." I bump her shoulder with mine.

"Remember how you asked me if Daddy Roger ever did anything to me?"

Oh no. Is she going to tell me something different now? "Yes?"

"Well… My real daddy did, and that's why he's in jail."

"What did your real daddy do?"

"He and his friends hurt me." She pointed to her girl parts.

"I know what you mean. That happened to me, too, in my past foster homes."

Her eyes get big. "Really?"

I put my arm around her. "I won't let anything happen to you. We are definitely going to stick together." I hold up my pinky. "Deal?"

"Deal." She does the same and we wrap them around each other's.

"We are SnowStorm together and we have to watch out for each other."

"Yes, we are, Anna. We are SnowStorm."

"Hey, we better get downstairs. Momma Jane sent me up here to wake you up."

"Is she a nice lady? Because she seems mean and grumpy a lot already."

"She's okay. She yells and throws our stuff away, but she hasn't hit me."

"That's good to know." I take her hand, my fingers winding with hers, and we leave the room. Just as we reach the top of the stairs, the house comes alive with noise—shouts, laughter, and the banging of dishes—clearly the rest of the family is downstairs, so I figure it's time for me to meet them.

Chapter 4
Marlene

I stop dead in the kitchen doorway as I stare at everyone sitting at the table, looking like one big *happy* family. Except for Jane, everyone turns their heads toward me, eyes wide, studying me like they're getting ready for a test. I hate this—sitting at the table with strangers who act like I belong, like I'm part of their family. It's pointless to fit in when I know I'll be moving again soon. This is their world, not mine.

I'm just here, hanging out in the doorway. For a moment, I shiver with nerves like I'm standing in the snow with no shoes. Why am I nervous? I should be used to this by now—moving all the time.

I shake off the feeling. I don't like to feel sad or nervous. Being weak is not an option. I have to be strong to survive my awful life in foster care.

"Yuck. Is that our new foster kid? She's ugly."

"Marlene, be nice." Jane tickles the girl's head as she walks by her.

Marlene looks around the table. "I'm glad there's no empty seat next to me."

I glare at her. I'm not afraid of anyone. Marlene and me, we are going to have some words. "I'm glad I don't have to sit next to you, either. I can smell you all the way over here."

Roger, Jenna, and Barry watch us. Jenna laughs. Then everyone else around the table does, too, except for Jane.

"I told you, Jane, that we have a sassy one," Roger says.

"We'll see how long that lasts."

Jane's words are a warning, I think. I'll have to watch out for her.

"Mom, are you going to let that foster kid talk to me that way? I'm your daughter and you better stick up for me!" Marlene yells at her mother.

I step into the room. "I'm glad to see you're smarter than you look. Yes. I *am* the new foster kid."

Marlene glares at me.

Mission accomplished. I think I'm going to enjoy making that snob mad.

"Enough, Anna. Get in here and grab a seat, and keep your smart words to yourself." Jane walks to an empty seat and pulls it out.

I'm not going to sit down as long as she's standing behind it. Jenna says she doesn't hit, but I'm not going to take any chances.

"There's room for you next to me, Anna." Jenna pulls me to the other side of the table.

As everyone goes back to their conversations, I'm left feeling as though I'm an outsider because even Jenna is laughing with Barry, the six-year-old foster boy who lives here, too.

"Hey, sweetie, do you want another bun?" Jane is all sweet and even winks at him.

Yup, he's her favorite.

"Yes! Ye!" Barry bounces in his seat.

This family has three foster kids, plus they do emergency placements. I know that a family gets paid for letting us stay with them; they must make a lot of money.

Jane acts nicer to Barry, and it doesn't take long to see that she gives him way more attention than she does to Jenna. She doesn't call her or me "sweetie."

"Jenna, how long has Barry lived here?"

Jenna takes a bite and then turns toward me. "Since he was a baby. They're going to adopt him." A noodle slides out of her mouth, but she pushes it back in.

"Adopt? What's that?"

"We are going to make Barry part of our family." Jane kisses Barry's cheek.

"How can you do that when he's a foster kid?"

Jane scowls like she's mad at me for asking a question. "It's called adoption, Anna. Once the court says Barry is ours, then he's our son and part of our family forever."

"Are you going to adopt us, too?" I point to Jenna and me.

"Absolutely not. Just Barry." Jane's lips turn down.

Is she grinning at me? Does it make her happy to tell me she doesn't want us?. "Good. I don't want to be adopted, anyway." I cock my head and push my nose up. My head tilt is my sassy, stubborn anger sign, something that always made my daddy in the first foster home chuckle. I want to make sure to show Jane that I'm not happy with her. I have a mean streak, too, and I'm not afraid to show it when someone is being mean to me first. And Jane was being mean.

"Anna, that's enough. No need to be rude." Roger sets his fork down hard.

"Jane's being rude, not me!" I roar at Roger. I'm tired of people being mean to me. I won't take it anymore.

That's it. I'm outta here. "I don't feel hungry." I stand.

"Excuse me? Where do you think you're going, young lady?" Jane yells.

I ignore her and push in my chair, then walk around the table to where Barry sits.

"Hi, Barry. I'm Anna." My hand hovers in front of his face while he stares.

I wave my hand again. "This means you're supposed to shake."

Barry smiles and grabs my hand. "Nice to meet you."

"Don't talk to her!" Marlene yells at him. "Why do we have to have these dirty foster kids anyway, Mother?"

Jane turns and plays with Marlene's hair. "Do you like your fancy pink bedroom?"

Marlene nods.

"Well, then, let me tell you where that money comes from." Jane points to me and Jenna. "It comes from us taking care of them."

So, the money that should be used for Jenna and me is, instead, used to make a fancy bedroom for the mean girl, while we sleep on an old, rickety bunk bed. That's not right.

"Since we paid for the pink room, shouldn't Jenna and I be the ones sleeping in it, not Marlene?" I stare at Jane.

"If you keep sassing me, you'll sleep in the basement. Go sit back down in your chair," Jane snaps.

I do as she says and sit back down next to my new foster sister. *What does she mean about the basement?*

Jenna squeezes my leg. "Anna, stop. You don't want to sleep in the dirty basement," she whispers.

"That's right. Listen to your foster sister, and keep your mouth shut if you know what's good for you." Jane slams her plate on the table.

"That's enough, Jane," Roger says. "Everyone has a bedroom, so there's no need to switch things around. I'm sure our foster girls didn't mean any harm." He winks at us.

Jane's face turns bright red. "I'm sick of you always sticking up for the foster girls. You stick up for them more than you do your own damn daughter." She glares at Roger.

Marlene whines, "Yes, Daddy, why are they your special girls and I'm not?"

"That's enough, all of you. Let's eat the spaghetti and then everyone can go outside to play. It's cold, but not enough that you can't get out." Roger rolls his spaghetti around his fork.

That's kinda groovy. I've never seen it done that way. But that doesn't mean I want to stay here with that creep. "I'm going to my room since I'm not hungry." I walk toward the door, but Roger blocks me when he sticks out his arm.

"You won't be doing that," he says, as I jerk away from his touch. "In this house, you ask to be excused from the table, and you wait until the entire family is finished eating.

"Fine!" I stomp back to my seat. I've never heard a dumber rule. I won't ask. I'm gonna sit here all day if I have to. Why should I bother being nice to them? I don't like them already. Maybe I need to come up with another plan to get outta here, like I did in my last foster home.

We're all quiet for the rest of dinner. Marlene gives me a dirty look, which I happily return. I know how to handle myself in foster care, so that snotty redhead better not start anything with me.

Roger's chair scrapes against the floor as he stands up. "I'm going to watch the news, Mother. Kids, get outside to play while you can. There are only a few hours of daylight left."

Marlene jumps up, running to hug her father. "I don't want to, Daddy, because it's too cold for me," She has an annoying baby voice. Ugh.

Roger rubs her head. "No problem, sweetie. Go upstairs and play with your dolls."

He's seriously weird. I get chills.

"Anna, do you want to go outside and play with me?" Jenna grabs my hand again.

I pull my hand away as Marlene watches.

"You two are weird, always holding hands. Do all foster kids act like freaks?" She laughs.

I step toward Marlene. I'm going to punch this girl in the face, and I don't care who's around or what happens to me.

But, suddenly, I stumble backward as Jenna pulls my hand again.

"Anna, come *on* and let's go outside."

I hesitate, sending Marlene an *I hate you* look before I leave.

"Yes, get outside and play for a while so I can clean up." Jane turns away from us and heads to the sink.

Ha. She forgot that I didn't ask to be excused. At least I know that this foster mother forgets things.

Once we're outside, Jenna says, "Marlene's not worth it. I said that Jane won't hit us but, I didn't say she wouldn't send you to bed without food or make you stay in your room for a few days with only one meal a day. Or, worse, make you sleep in the creepy dirt basement with the door locked."

I drop Jenna's hand as we stop on the edge of the sidewalk. "Well, that's good information to have." Though, honestly, I've been through worse so that's not gonna stop me from hitting Marlene.

How long have these people been doing foster care? I guess we *are* just a job to them. For a second, I put my head down.

Jenna tugs on my arm as she drags me to the end of the driveway, then points to an enormous stone building. "Are you excited about school tomorrow? We live so close we can walk."

"Nope. I don't like school."

Jenna plops down onto the grass, with her legs crossed. She pats the earth for me to join her. "What grade are you in?"

"Fifth grade. Well, I think, but I don't really know. I've moved so much since school started that I can't keep track."

Jenna looks sad. "I'm in fourth grade because I failed last year. I'm dumb."

That's how I feel all the time. "No, you're not. You get to learn things again so you will remember it forever."

"Who needs to remember math forever." We both laugh.

She picks up a piece of straw from the grass and begins twisting it as she talks. "How many times have you moved?

I think for a second to make sure I can keep it all straight. "I lived with my first daddy, Sue & Allen, Jessica, Mrs. Dorsey, Momma Johnson, Georgia & Frank, and now—here."

"That's a lot of places. It's only the last week in September."

"Oh, you mean this year since school started?"

"Yeah."

"Um. Mrs. Dorsey for a few weeks. Then I moved to live with Momma Johnson. She made the best food." The smell of her cooking was so good. "Next, I moved to live with Georgia and Frank. But I was only there a few nights. She's the one that had the beating room I told you about. And now I'm here."

"That's a lot, Anna." Jenna grabs my hand.

"I know. No one seems to want me." For a moment, I'm sad, because it's just plain sad to be all alone. But then I shake my shoulders. "But that's okay; I don't need anyone, anyway."

I don't want to think about this anymore right now.

Jenna puts her finger on her chin. "Well, you might not need anyone, but I like to have nice people around. Come with me. I have an idea." She jumps up. "Let's roll down the hill together." She lays flat on the grass. "See, Anna? Copy me."

Down the hill she rolls. And so, do I. The world spins so fast that I have to close my eyes.

"Isn't that so much fun, Anna?"

I stand up slowly but then I fall down.

Jenna laughs, wrapping her arms around her stomach.

"That was actually really cool!" I laugh so hard I think I may pee my pants. Why didn't I ever think of rolling down a hill? "Let's do it again!"

"Okay, but let's roll down together this time and find out who can reach the bottom first."

"Great idea!"

Just Another Door

Jenna reminds me of my brother, Curtis, because she likes playing games and is competitive, just like him. That's what he and I did all the time when we were locked out at my first foster home. He'd love this game. How I wish he was here, rolling down the grass bank with us. *I miss you, Curtis.*

I lie down on the ground, my head next to Jenna's, then we roll down the hill faster and faster, 'til we reach the bottom.

"Jenna, I'm having so much fun!" My sides ache from laughing so hard as I watch Jenna try to stand."

"You two!" Jane yells from the window. "Come in the house and get ready for a bath, so you can go to bed for school tomorrow."

Jenna gets a weird look on her face. "I hate bath night. Sometimes, Roger and Jane take turns checking to make sure I've washed."

Right away, Derek pops into my head, and I remember screaming at my first foster mother that I could wash myself. Derek only wanted to bathe me so he could hurt me. "You're big enough to give yourself a bath."

"I told them that, but they don't listen to me." Jenna looks down at the grass.

"Well, don't you worry about it. Let's come up with a plan for bath time."

Jenna jumps up, clapping. "Okay, Anna, what's the plan?"

I inch closer, my heart pounding because I'm worried Jane might eavesdrop from the back window. I lean into Jenna and whisper, "We will be in the bathroom together tonight when both of us take a bath."

Jenna looks down. "Um… okay."

I take a deep breath. "This way, if Roger's in the bathroom, we can keep an eye on him and yell for help if anything happens."

"Okay, Anna. We better get back into the house, so Momma Jane doesn't have to come out and look for us." She grabs my hand—boy, this girl really likes to hold hands. "She blows a fuse when she has to hunt us down." She practically drags me to the house.

Holding her hand will take some getting used to because I don't wanna hurt her feelings by telling her to stop.

We are barely in the house before Jane meets us at the door. Was she just standing there, waiting for us?

"Jenna, why don't you take a bath first. It's Roger's turn to help you girls this evening."

Is the woman crazy? Why is she okay with her husband watching us in the bathroom?

"Jane, Jenna and I don't need Roger's help in the bathroom," I snap.

Jane's eyes widened, like two big, surprised bugs. "Who mentioned Daddy Roger being in the bathroom with you? And I've told you before to call us Momma Jane and Daddy Roger.

"Then why did you say that, Roger… is going to help us tonight with baths?"

She plants her hands on her hips, a determined and frustrated expression on her face, as she bites her lips before talking again. "You ask a lot of damn questions." She rubs her temples. "After you leave the bathroom, I want Roger to smell your hair to confirm you washed it and didn't just stand in the shower, pretending."

"Why would someone do that?" Oh, wait—I for sure would try to get away with it. I can't stand being in the bathroom, especially since that's where I have to get washed up. I sometimes think about Derek and what he did to me while I'm in the bath. If I could trick a foster parent into thinking I took a bath, I would totally do it. This foster mother might be a smart one if she knows that trick.

"Anna, enough questions. Go get your pajamas, both of you, and get a shower or a bath, whichever you prefer."

As Jenna and I walk upstairs, we hear Roger come in the door. "Is it my turn tonight to verify showers?"

"Sure is. I've got to clean up the mess in the kitchen."

"Sweetheart, wouldn't it be easier if the girls took a bath?"

"Roger, I'm fine with whatever the girls do, as long as they're clean."

Right before we get to our bedroom, Roger yells from downstairs, "Time for a bath, ladies! I'll come by to make sure you're squeaky clean!"

There's that word—*clean*. That's what Derek had said he was doing when he'd checked a certain part of my body to make sure it was clean. I feel like I want to throw up all over Jenna's bottom bunk.

"Jenna, let me know when you're ready, then we'll go into the bathroom together." I grab my PJs. This will be new for me, taking a bath with a foster sister in the room, but I'd rather it be her than any boy.

"Got 'em. Let's go, Anna." She locks her arm in mine like we're on the yellow brick road.

I hold Jenna's towel for her. "Be careful. Don't get the water too hot.

I hate when that happens." Boy, *do* I. I've been burned by water more than I want to think about.

The big white tub has feet on it, holding it off the ground. It looks like a tiger ready to attack us any minute. There is no way to make any bathtub look pretty no matter what kind of feet you put on it.

When Jenna starts to undress, I turn around and pretend I'm pulling at the ugly green wallpaper with purple flowers. "How's the water, Jenna?" I feel weird being here with her because I know how much I hate it when someone's in the bathroom with me. But we have to keep each other safe.

"You can turn around, Anna. I'm in the water."

I spin around and grab a washcloth. "Let's put this over the hole in the door so no one can see us."

"Yes, Anna. I never thought of that."

As soon as the towels in place, I sit on the toilet.

"Our schools are next to each other, so we can walk together." Jenna's sounds happy.

I look around the room, still not wanting to watch Jenna in the tub. "That'd be…" I freeze because I notice the bathroom doorknob moving slightly.

"Great, Jenna. I can't wait for school tomorrow!" My voice booms through the bathroom so I can make sure that the person on the other side of the door will hear me and go away.

"Anna, why—?"

I put a finger to my lips and point at the door.

She nods. "The kids here are super friendly! You'll love them!" she shouts back.

Footsteps disappear down the hall.

We both sigh with relief.

"I think your plan worked, Anna."

I think so too. At least, for now.

But now it's my turn for a bath, and I don't want to get undressed in front of anyone, not even a girl. But it would be way worse if Roger walked in while I was alone in the bathroom, so I'm gonna have to. Better to be naked in front of Jenna than Roger.

I make it quick, then get dressed and ready for whatever happens next in this home.

I move the washcloth from the doorknob. When I open the door, I find Roger standing there. "Anna, you nearly hit me with the door!" What was he up to, hunched over by the bathroom door handle?

"Sorry." That's all I'm saying, because maybe he shouldn't have been standing there.

"Let me sniff your heads." He takes a good whiff of Jenna's hair. "Ooh, you smell so good and fresh." He stands up again. "Anna, you're up!"

I step backward. "I don't need you to smell my hair because, as you can see, my hair's still wet."

"I understand that, but I must check it for myself." He points to his nose.

"Nope, I'm not going to let you do that." I stomp my foot.

"Anna Snow, get over here so I can make sure, and then the two of you can be off to bed. Trust me, the last thing you want is for Mother to find out you refused; she'll be furious. That creepy, dark basement even freaks *me* out, especially with that furnace that looks like a place where they'd burn bodies. There's a mountain of dirt, and we heard there are coffins under all of it." Roger leans closer to my face with a weird smile. "I'd hate for you to spend the night down there, locked up all alone. Which is what'll happen if you tell me no." That smile turns into a smirk.

Ha. He thinks he can scare me? The guy doesn't know what I've been through. "I don't care. I'll spend the night with dead people before I let you smell my hair."

His sudden movement is a blur—one minute I'm standing there, and the next, he yanks me up against him and inhales my hair.

I swing out with my arms, flailing wildly like a cat trying to scratch something, to get away. As I swing them at him in a desperate attempt to break free, he lets go.

"All of that was unnecessary. You smell clean. See? Was that so hard and did it require all that fighting?"

I turn my back on him. I can't look at Roger right now because I think I'm gonna puke. He just touched me when I didn't want him to. Why do boys think they can do whatever they want to girls? Why?

"Enough with all this drama. Get into bed." He walks away then and heads down the stairs.

Good riddance.

"Anna, you don't want to spend the night in the basement. I had to do it once, and it was super scary. That big furnace is noisy, and I swear

I saw ghosts everywhere. It was so dark down there except for a little bit of light coming through the window. It was hard to see." She shivers.

"I don't care, Jenna. That man is way creepier than a basement could ever be."

"I don't know about that, Anna. You haven't seen it down there yet, and I hope you never have to."

"Let's go to bed and make sure we face the door so we can see if anyone tries to come into our room." I don't mention that I'd seen Roger looking at me while I was asleep earlier because I don't want to scare her. But me? I'm more angry than scared. He better not try anything.

I move Raggedy to the outside of my bed, so I can cuddle her as I watch the door at the same time. Her red hair tickles my nose.

What a day, Jesus. I'm talking to you in my head so no one else can hear me except you. Please watch over me and Jenna. I can tell that she's scared, too. Keep Roger and that nasty Marlene away from us—but, most importantly, Roger. I get a feeling he's not a good man and might like to hurt little girls. Please watch out for us. Goodnight, Jesus. Amen.

Chapter 5
Small Bear

"Wake up, Anna! We're going to be late for school!"

Jenna's voice jolts me out of my sleep.

By the time I roll over, I see Jenna standing at my bed dressed in shorts and a T-shirt.

"C'mon, Anna!" She claps her hands like a cheerleader at school. "I put your clothes up on your bunk. Momma Jane got them out for you last night. Shorts. We get to wear them today because it's going to be hot." She spins in a circle like she's dancing.

How can she be so happy about school? It's an awful place that reminds me of how dumb I really am. I'm not good at it at *all*.

Breakfast with the new foster family is better than dinner. No one takes the time to talk to each other. We gobble down eggs and bacon before heading to the front door.

Jane stands with brown bags for all of us. "You both have a peanut butter and jelly sandwich, apples, and milk. Have a good day."

"'Bye, Momma Jane. See you later." Jenna skips down the house steps.

Just Another Door

"'Bye, Jane. Thanks for the sandwich. Are you not taking me to school today since it's my first day?"

"Have a good day, Anna, and I think you can do this on your own," Jane whispers as she hands me the bag

I twist around to see her hugging and kissing Marlene. "My sweet girl. I'm so proud and love you so much. Have a great day at school."

Yuck. Though, honestly? I wish I had a mother who loved me like that.

"Come on, Anna! You don't want to be late for school!" Jenna yells from the end of the driveway.

My head swings back around to see Jenna hopping in place like a rabbit. Can't that girl stand still?

"I can't wait to tell my teacher that I have a new foster sister."

"That's nice, Jenna."

"What's wrong, Anna? You're quiet." Jenna kicks a small rock on the sidewalk.

"I hate going to a new school. It sucks." The teachers always make me stand in front of the class to introduce myself, like I'm a toy for show-and-tell. It's like they're telling everyone I'm a rejected, unwanted foster kid. I hate it. I wish Jenna was in my grade and my class because that would make things easier for me. But she's in fourth grade and still goes to elementary school. I'm happy that we can walk together, since our schools are right next to each other. That's better than walking all by myself.

"I'm sorry, Anna. Maybe you'll get a cool teacher like mine."

"I doubt that. "Bye, Jenna, I'll see you on the way home." My foster sister goes off in one direction as I go into another. *Middle School here I come.*

Everyone crowds around the door trying to get into the building and I'm no different.

"Move out of the way!" a tall boy screams as he bumps into me, making me drop my lunch bag.

Just as I bend over to pick it up, someone else pushes me and I fall on the hallway floor.

"Hurry and move it!" someone else shouts.

Move it? To where should I move it? I have no idea where I'm going since Jane didn't want to bring me today.

My breathing changes, acting as though I'm running a race. Where the heck am I supposed to go? I spin in circles in the middle of the hallway in front of the office. I guess I should go in and ask someone.

Dr. Sharon Zaffarese-Dippold

A girl stops and asks, "Are you lost?"

"Yeah. I'm tryin' to find fifth grade."

"You're close. It's right there." She points to the door. "'Bye."

She vanishes into the crowd of kids as quickly as she'd arrived.

The classroom is noisy while I wait by the door for the teacher to assign me a seat. Kids walk by, staring at me. Having been the new kid more times than I can count, I know exactly what to expect.

While I wait for the teacher, Marlene walks past me and into the classroom. I'm always running away from bullies in my dreams. Now one of those people is in my class. Seriously? It's like my bad dreams are happening in real life. This is crap.

Marlene looks at me, then sticks her tongue out. "Really? I have to have the ugly girl in my class?"

If I had thought about it sooner, I would've put my foot out to trip her. Darn it! Too bad she's already standing far away from me. Maybe I can just knock her over—but that wouldn't be such a good impression on the first day of school. But then, when did I ever care about what others thought of me in school?

"Who's the new girl standing by the door?" a boy asks, bringing me out of my thoughts.

Marlene rolls her eyes. "She's the nasty new foster kid living with us. She smells horrible." Marlene plugs her nose and smiles.

Argh. That girl. Now the students know I'm a foster kid. Thanks, Marlene. I want to punch her so badly right now.

"Anna, come stand by me so I can introduce you to the class," the teacher says to me.

Here we go—my entire life story is about to be told to a bunch of kids I have no idea who they are…

I clench my fists, getting ready for the embarrassing introductions from the teacher. Some tell the kids more information than others, but the end is always the same: I'm a freak show. My nails dig deeper. I don't even feel the pain from it.

The teacher claps her hands together. Everyone jumps, including me. "Please find your seats, everyone, so we can begin today's math assignments."

The room feels alive with the kids moving around, the rustle of papers, and the whispers of conversations still happening as everyone walks to their desks.

Just Another Door

A girl with short, dark hair stands in front of me. "Who are you?"

"I'm Anna."

"Wow, we almost have the same name. My name is Anna-Marie." She reaches for my hand, but I pull back. It doesn't stop this girl from talking, though. "I go by Marie." Her smile is so wide that her back teeth are showing.

Because I move around so much, being able to trust people stopped working inside of me. But this girl seems nice enough.

"Marie, take your seat, please, and give Anna Snow some room."

Marie moves fast, her feet barely making a sound on the squeaky floor. There's an empty seat behind her, and there's another behind Marlene and another behind a boy at the back. Here's hoping I get to sit behind Marie.

"Class, let's give a warm welcome to Anna Snow. She moved here from Fennedy, which is a much smaller school, so let's help her out today in the hallway to get to her other classes." She smiles at me. "Please follow me to my desk, where I will provide you with the necessary notebook and pencil for your note-taking."

Note-taking? What the heck is that?

The teacher opens her desk, then hands me the things. "My name is Mrs. Swing." She leans close to me and whispers, "I put you behind Marie because I didn't think you'd want to sit around any mean kids. Marie will help you out."

Phew. "Thanks, Mrs. Swing." I walk to my chair, glad that my teacher didn't tell the kids that I was a foster child. In fact, she said nothing bad and actually asked the students to help me. Mrs. Swing might be all right. Maybe this school will be a better place than the foster home.

As soon as I sit down on my wooden chair, Marlene's voice squashes my ideas. "Thank you, Mrs. Swing, for putting that dirty foster kid on the other side of the classroom away from me. I have to live with her, and that's bad enough."

I snap my head to glare at her across the room.

She smirks and laughs out loud so everyone can hear it.

Other kids join her.

"Enough, Marlene!" Mrs. Swing's reprimand echoes through the classroom. She walks to Marlene's desk. "Stand up, young lady. I'll be moving you to the hallway for the morning since you aspire to be mean to another student. Let's see how you like it out there." She drags Marlene's desk to the door.

Marlene glares back at me.

Mrs. Swing drops the desk, but she doesn't look away from Marlene. "Anyone else feeling like joining her, just keep laughing, and I'll send you all to the principal's office and call your parents."

Wow. I didn't know a teacher could send the whole class to the principal. Mrs. Swing is a badass.

The room gets quiet.

"That's better. Now, get out your math assignment as I get Marlene set up in the hallway."

The desk's legs scrape against the floor, each screech sending a shiver down my spine; it sounds like nails on a chalkboard as Mrs. Swing drags it out the door.

Marie turns around. "Woohoo. Mrs. Swing told Marlene off. It's about time someone put that nasty girl in her place." Marie giggles.

I can't believe this new teacher—who doesn't even know me—has my back! Maybe I'll finally like school. It'd be nice to like my teacher again—like I liked Mrs. Young at my first foster home. She made up a birthday for me because I don't know when my birthday is. She even threw me a fake birthday party at school so I could have a party like the rest of the kids. Which reminds me, I'm gonna have to ask Jane when it is.

Mrs. Swing walks back into the classroom toward Marie and me.

She taps Marie's desk. "Marie and Anna Snow, how about you both move your desks to the back and sit together?"

She wants us to do what? I thought teachers didn't like kids to sit together because they can talk too much.

"Marie, you can help Anna Snow get caught up on what we are working on. But, please, keep your voices down." She smiles at us both, then walks to the chalkboard.

Jenna and my desks scrape the floor as we move them to the back of the other seats and put them side-by-side.

"This is so cool. You're my desk partner." Marie seems happy about this.

Maybe I am, too. For once, I'm not sitting alone, feeling clueless. I'm really grateful that my teacher set up Marie to help me.

Mrs. Swing writes a fraction on the board. "Do I have a volunteer for a peer group to come forward to work on the math problem?"

I stare at the numbers. I wish I was good at math, but when I see math problems, my heart races for no reason.

I sorta remember this fraction thing from my old school, but I wasn't there long enough to learn how to do it. I put my head down—a strategy I learned a long time ago. *Don't look at a teacher who has a question, because they will call on you.*

"Yes, Marie. Why don't you and Anna Snow both come up, then?"

What? Is she serious? I pick my head up and look at Marie to find her hand straight in the air. Yikes! And Marie is already standing up and waving for me to follow her before I can even say a word.

"Let's go, Anna! We got this."

I look around, and the entire class is staring.

Slowly, I follow Marie to the green chalkboard, the squeak of my shoes echoing in the quiet room.

Mrs. Swing hands each of us a piece of chalk, then walks away while Marie and I think about the math problem—well, while *Marie* does. Me? I just freeze, every muscle in my body stiffening with fear. "Marie," I whisper, "this problem looks hard; I have no idea how to do it."

She smiles at me. "Don't worry, Anna Snow. I can do it."

Then she actually does, her piece of chalk flying across the board as she solves the darn thing. Clearly, she doesn't need my help. Which is a good thing because we'd be here 'til next week solving this thing if it was up to me.

Marie turns to face the class, and I follow her lead.

"Anna Snow, do you want to change Marie's answer, or do you agree with your partner?" Mrs. Swing asks.

I slowly look at the math problem, shrug, then say to Mrs. Swing, "It looks right to me."

Marie and I look at the class while the teacher checks Marie's answer. In the back row, a kid who'd been chatting with Marlene earlier, makes bunny sounds.

Of *course* he's picking on my teeth. I wonder if he'd find it funny if I walked to his desk and knocked *his* front teeth out?

"Enough, Jimmy. I can hear you up here, so you'll be joining your friend, Marlene, in a second."

Jimmy shuts up, and it's all I can do not to stick my tongue out at him. But I don't want to get in trouble like he is.

"Great job, girls. Please head back to your desks."

Did a teacher just tell me I did a great job? I didn't do anything. Marie did all the work.

"Thank you, Marie. I had no clue how to solve that math problem. I haven't learned it yet."

"No worries, Anna Snow. I'll help you," she says, her voice barely above a whisper.

I mirror her smile, feeling happy for the moment. It's nice to have a friend at a new school.

Finally, it's time for recess.

Marie stands at the door and yells down the hallway at me, "Come on, Anna Snow! We can play hopscotch!"

"What the heck is hopscotch?" I ask as we head outside.

"You'll see. Just follow me."

I do as she says, then take a rock that she hands me after she divides a bunch of us into teams.

"Okay, Anna Snow. You're on our team, The Bugs."

"Um. Marie? Who came up with that name?" What an awful name for a team.

"I did." She smiles real big. "Do you like it?"

I don't want to hurt her feelings since she's been so nice to me, so I lie. It's not bad to lie if it's to not hurt someone's feelings. "Ah. Sure. The Bugs, it is."

She explains the game to me. Not sure I get the whole thing, but I'll learn as I go along. After all, I'm good at figuring stuff out in the moment. I've had to do that since this whole foster kid thing started."

My heart pounds like a gigantic drum against my ribs. The thought of these kids' making fun of me makes my stomach burn like it's on fire.

"All right, Anna Snow, let's go!"

Marlene steps forward. "Let's beat these nasty girls."

I really don't like bullies, and I really don't like Marlene. But I really like challenges, so she's gonna be sorry for that comment in class.

Side-by-side, Marlene and Marie toss their rocks, the sound of each impact echoing against the pavement. Marie's rock lands on square 9, but Marlene's rock bounces and skips, landing not on one of the squares, but into the grass.

You show her, Marie!

Marie jumps up and down. "The Bugs go first!"

No matter what we do, our team can't get a break.

Marlene's team smokes us. Not a single one on their team lost a point.

Marlene gets in Marie's face. "Great name for your team, Marie. *Bugs*. We smashed you like the gross bugs you are."

I step forward, ready to attack, but then the bell rings to go back to class.

I feel a soft tap on my shoulder and turn to find Marie shaking her head. "Anna Snow, she's not worth it. Let's go."

My new friend and I walk back to class side-by-side. Which is a good thing, since I have no clue yet how to get around at this new school. I like the sound of calling her my friend. I hope she doesn't get mad and stop talking to me, leaving me alone at school. Foster parents move me when they're angry, so friends certainly can, too.

Marlene bumps into my shoulder as she walks past me through the door. "Don't embarrass me, scum bag."

"You're the scumbag, not me," I snarl at her.

Marlene walks back up to me.

I turn my back to the chalkboard and square off face-to-face with this mean girl I have to live with. I'm just about to tell her off when a hand lands on my arm.

"Marlene, that's enough," My teacher says.

"Of course, Mrs. Swing." Marlene squeals back, her voice so high it hurts my ears. She's trying to be so sweet talking to the teacher..

"Anna, please take your seat."

I don't want to—I really want to beat the piss out of Marlene—but Mrs. Swing has been kind to me, so I do as she says.

Marie turns around as soon as I sit down. "Marlene sucks. I'm sorry you have to live with her."

"Yeah, me, too." If my new friend had any clue about all the awful people I've had to live with, she'd know that Marlene is just another one of them.

Mrs. Swing walks in front of the chalkboard. "Okay, class, let's get our family art projects out. Who would like to go first?"

Family projects? What the heck am I supposed to do with this? I don't have one—a project *or* a family. School shouldn't make you feel like garbage, but this project does. Now, I have to sit and listen to how great everyone's families are?

"I'll go first, Mrs. Swing!" Marlene yells. Why does she have to be the center of attention?

"Okay, Marlene. Come up front to show the class your family."

Marlene turns her picture around and points to her parents, then to

Dr. Sharon Zaffarese-Dippold

Barry. "This is my little brother, Barry. My parents are adopting him because he doesn't have a family. He's lived with us since he was born."

"That's nice of your family, Marlene." My teacher sounds kind. "Who else is in your picture?"

"This is Anna Snow. She lives with us because no one else wants her. My family takes in reject kids."

Some of the kids laugh because of *course* she drew me with big buck teeth. I hate my teeth. I hate my one eyebrow. I hate being me. Why would the other kids think it's funny to not have a family?

Mrs. Swing marches over to Marlene, eyes blazing, and rips the picture from her hands, writes something on it really fast, then turns it around for the rest of us to see. "*This* is what happens when you make fun of someone in my room." There's a big, red *F* on the paper. "Marlene, you fail this project for being mean to another student. Sit down. I'm sure your mother will not be happy about this."

I'm sure she won't be either; Jane is a witch. But… who knows? Marlene seems spoiled to me, so maybe nothing will happen to her. But at least I got to see her get the *F*, and I know she's not happy with it or that I saw it. Which makes my day. Serves her right for being mean.

Mrs. Swing sets Marlene's picture down on her desk. "Class, we'll finish up with the projects later. Right now, work on your spelling words." She looks at me. "Anna Snow, can you come to my desk, please?"

Oh, great. What did I do now?

I walk slowly to where my teacher sits. Is this going to be a whipping about all the bad things I've done since I've been here? Did she figure out that I'm just plain dumb?

Mrs. Swing points to an empty chair. "Take a seat, sweetheart."

My legs bounce up and down because I'm nervous. Thankfully, my teacher's desk keeps the other kids from seeing me—I hate people staring at me.

Mrs. Swing leans close to my chair, then whispers, "I was a foster kid, too."

I jerk back away from her. "You were?"

"Yup. I was made fun of because of foster care—I'm not going to let the kids in this class do the same thing to you." She bumps my shoulder like friends do with each other. "We foster kids have to stick together." She winks. "But… that doesn't mean you are exempt from doing the work in my class; I expect you to complete all assignments."

She opens her desk drawer. "I'll send you to a quiet study hall at the end of the day, where you can focus on your work, and I can also set up a tutor for extra help if you'd like."

She looks at me so hard that I'm not sure what she wants me to do.

"You were a foster kid, too?" I ask again because I'm still shocked that she lived in foster care; I never would've guessed a *teacher* could have been unwanted... like me.

"Being a foster kid shouldn't stop you from achieving your dreams." She points to all the kids. "You might live differently than they do, but that doesn't have to stop you. You can do and be anything you want to. Don't forget that. But you have to work hard to do it—maybe even harder than the rest of the class. So... do you want me to set you up with study hall at the end of the day with a tutor—someone to help you?"

"Um...." I don't want anyone to help me because the rest of the kids in class will think I'm stupid—which I am, but I don't want other kids to know that. I'm dumb when it comes to schoolwork. Does Mrs. Swing know that, too, and is that why she wants me to work with someone? "Why do I have to work harder than the kids in the class?"

"Because they have people and families to help them, but you might not have the same support. Does that make sense?"

"Ohhh." That makes me feel better. I have to work harder because I'm a foster kid, *not* because I'm stupid. Mrs. Swing doesn't think that I'm horrible at school, but she'll find out soon enough. "Can I just do the study hall and not have someone help me?" If the kids see someone with me, they'll laugh, so I definitely don't want that. "Where would I have study hall?"

"The study room is in the office, next to the front desk." She stops talking to write a note.

I peek back at the kids, just barely poking my head over the half-wall to make sure no one's watching or listening to us. They're all busy doing something else, even Marlene. Good.

I turn back around to see Mrs. Swing watching me.

"No one will know you're in the study room. I'll tell the class that you are the office helper and your job is to take paperwork to the principal's office at the end of the day. Everyone has some kind of responsibility in the classroom. Even Marie cleans the erasers so, no one will question anything."

I nod. If no one finds out I need special help, what do I have to lose? But if the kids *do* find out, that's it for me.

"Also, Anna, I realize that not all foster homes are nice." She pats my hand. "I'm here if you need to talk to someone."

Our eyes lock together for a second, one foster child to another.

"Okay." The foster kid thing is still blowing my mind; I don't know what to say.

"Great. I think study hall will be helpful to you. We'll start tomorrow."

"Okay." I'm not as sure about it as Mrs. Swing, but it's nice that she's trying to help me. I'm not used to that.

"Head back to your seat, since it's almost time for dismissal."

Marie turns to me when I slide behind my desk. "Anna Snow, are you okay? You were up there a long time. Are you in trouble?"

"No. Mrs. Swing just wanted to give me—"

"Wonderful news, everyone." My teacher interrupts what I was going to tell Marie. "Anna Snow will be our classroom liaison to the main office. She'll take all graded papers to the office staff at the end of the day."

"That's not fair!" Marlene says.

"That's enough, Marlene. You already have a job, passing around the handouts on Mondays and Fridays."

"Yeah, but that's boring as crap. Anna Snow gets to leave class. Why can't she pass out the handouts and *I* leave at the end of each day to talk to people in the main office?" Marlene flips her hair and kicks her desk leg.

"Again, Marlene, you already have a job for the year and that's what you chose."

This girl is seriously a brat. If she doesn't get her way, she gets mad at something or someone. I think she gets madder than I do.

The bell rings. "Bus riders, please line up by the door. You're excused."

Not thinking, I line up with everyone else.

Mrs. Swing hands me a notebook. "You forgot this. Aren't you a walker, Anna?"

"Oh yes, I am."

"Stupid!" Marlene snarls as she walks past me. "Mrs. Swing, if Anna Snow can't follow simple directions like lining up for a bus, how do you expect her to remember what to say to the people in the office?"

My teacher turns to Marlene. "It's tough for new students like Anna to adjust to a new school initially." She stares at her. "It was hard for you too, if I remember last year."

Marlene puts her nose in the air. Mrs. Swing moves so she's standing by the door.

As soon as Mrs. Swing isn't looking, Marlene sticks out her tongue at me.

I return the favor. I will not take her crap. I don't have to. I'm so tired of people thinking it's okay to bully or hurt me. I don't like this girl, so I'm going to be as mean to her as she is to me.

"Bye, Anna Snow!" Marie yells, waving as she leaves class with the bus riders.

"Walkers, line up, please. It's your turn to leave," Mrs. Swing announces.

I try to stay as far from Marlene as possible because I do *not* want to walk home with her. Even though it's not that far, any time spent with her is too much.

"Keep scumbag foster girl away from me, please. She might give me cooties." Marlene's voice carries across the room so everyone can hear. A burst of laughter rang out from the walkers.

Am I a scumbag? I look down at my clean legs. If she thinks I'm a scumbag now, she should've seen me in my first foster home; my legs were always dirty from making mud-pies. I let out a big breath. No matter what I do or how I look, people see me the same way—dirty.

"Don't worry, Marlene, she's in the back of the line," a girl behind Marlene says as she giggles.

I take a step out of line and spot Marlene. I'm going to lay her out flat right in front of everyone. Let's see her laugh then. I take two steps forward.

"Anna?" Mrs. Swing stands before me. "Sometimes it's better to look the other way. Maybe today is one of those times?" My teacher points to my place in line.

Then she turns to Marlene. "And, you, Marlene. If I hear any more about another student from you, you'll have after-school detention, and I'll talk to your mother."

Marlene mumbles, "Yeah. Whatever, teach," then hurries out.

Mrs. Swing stands by the door. "It's nice to meet you, Anna, and I look forward to seeing you tomorrow." She waves.

My teacher sounds like she likes me. That's the first.

I look for Jenna as soon as I'm by the road. Nothing. I don't see her yet. I might as well kick some stones as I walk back to the place I'm supposed to call home now,

One, two, three, kick. The stone soars through the air and lands in the parking lot. I skip to it, then kick it again. I wonder if my brother still kicks rocks or skips them in the creek like we use to—

Someone shoves me in my back and I fly to the ground. The only thing I can do to stop myself is to put my hands in front of me, hoping to protect my face.

It doesn't work. I end up lying on the concrete parking lot with stones in my mouth. My face and body hurt all over.

"Look at her now, lying on her ugly face. Don't you mess with me again, Miss Anna Snow."

I growl like a dog as I stand up and face Marlene. The girl made a big mistake letting me get free, and she's gonna find that out real soon. One of many things I learned in foster care is how to fight. *Let's go, prissy girl.* My fists are in front of my face and I'm ready to box.

"Ha! Look at you. Your face is all dirty." She points at me as her friends laugh.

I take a step closer.

"You need a bath, dirty girl. Don't you know how to clean yourself?" she says.

She doesn't have a clue how much danger she's in.

Bam! My fist lands on its target—one of Marlene's cheeks.

Then I smash the other.

Marlene screams, then falls to the ground and her friend's scatter.

They must not be such good friends since they leave her there. Serves her right.

I feel bad—well, for a second or two—that I hit her, but she pushed me first. She shouldn't have done that. I do *not* like people touching me, and I *especially* don't like people hurting me.

I walk ahead into the house, leaving Marlene on the concrete in the school parking lot—just like she would have left me—and I let the door slam behind me after I enter.

"Marlene, sweetheart," Jane calls out, "I have a cupcake waiting for you at the table."

"It's Anna."

"Anna?"

Just Another Door

"Yup." That's not what Jane wanted. She was hoping for her sweet Marlene. Well, her sweet Marlene will come in later with a broken face.

Jenna slams into me, making me drop my books, then she squeezes my waist.

Jane taps the tabletop. "Let go of Anna, Jenna, and get back to doing your homework. And, Anna, have a seat as well and get started on your schoolwork too."

"I don't have any homework. Can I just go to my room?"

Jame waves her hand. "Where's Marlene?"

I clear my throat. "I, uh, don't know where she is,"

"Huh. That's weird. She's usually home by now." Jane stops talking as the screen door opens behind me.

Marlene comes in crying. "Mom, look what Anna did to me." She points to her bloody lip."

"She's lying. I didn't punch her on the lip. She pushed me to the ground, so I punched her cheeks." I point to the cuts on the palms of my hand.

"My sweet girl. Let's get you cleaned up." Jane, of *course,* doesn't listen to me and, instead, wraps her arm around her daughter and leads her to the kitchen. And naturally, she screams at me. "Get upstairs, Anna, until I have time to talk to you."

"Mom, that girl is mean and has to leave. She's in my class and picked on me all day."

Marlene's voice fades as I get further up the steps. She's a liar. I don't care if they move me. I'm used to leaving places, anyway.

I scrunch up my face so much my cheeks hurt, then I dump the books onto the floor. I climb onto my bunk with Teddy and Raggedy. I actually *don't* want to move. I like my new teacher, and my new friend, Marie, is nice. I've never had a foster sister before. It might be worth it to live here with Marlene and the mean foster mother to have Jenna as a sister.

I wonder what this lady is going to do to me for beating up Marlene. Not that I really care—that girl deserved it. I'll worry about it later because I'm tired. I close my eyes and squeeze Teddy.

"Anna?"

I hear a whisper. My eyes flitter open. "Jenna? Is that you?"

"Yes, Anna. Wake up! Jane sounds pissed off. She said you broke Marlene's face."

"Right." I giggle.

"Anna, seriously. Marlene's face is all red and swollen." She stands on the bottom bunk so her head is over the top.

"Good. She deserves it."

"I know she does, but Jane is mad. Get up because she said she was coming upstairs to get you." Jenna hands me a small stuffed bear. "Tuck this in your belly so if you have to sleep in the basement tonight, you can lean this against the wall for a pillow." She pushes the bear over to me.

"Nah. I'm good." I shove the bear back, then sit up when I hear footsteps coming up the stairs. "Jenna? What time is it?"

"Late. We ate dinner already, and Jane said you were being punished tonight for beating up Marlene."

"*She* pushed *me*."

"Well, I don't think Jane's gonna—"

"Jenna, get yourself downstairs. I need to talk to Anna."

Yeah, Jenna's right; Jane's pissed.

As soon as Jenna leaves, Jane turns her red, angry face toward me, eyes narrowed, lips pursed in a tight line. "What the *hell* did you do to my daughter, and why do you think it's okay to punch her in the face?"

I hold out my hands to show her the cuts on my palms.

Jane looks for a second. "No matter. You do *not* put your hands on my child, do you hear me?" Jane's pointer finger is almost touching my nose. "Here." She hands me a sandwich. "This is all you're getting for dinner, and when you're finished, come downstairs because you're going to be sleeping in the basement tonight." She leaves the room, slamming the door behind her.

I look at the sandwich. Ha, joke's on her; peanut butter and jelly's my favorite.

I take a bite. This is better than anything she could have made for dinner.

As I swallow, Jane appears in my doorway. "Let's go."

I hold up my sandwich. "I didn't finish."

"That's not my fault. I told you to hurry up and eat it."

I jump off the bed and walk close to Jane—but not close enough that she can hit me.

"Hand me your plate and sandwich."

I sigh. "But I'm hungry. Can I eat it as I follow you?"

"No." She holds out her hand. "Give me your sandwich."

I place it in her hand.

Just Another Door

"Now, follow me."

Maybe I should've taken Jenna's offer of the bear.

I follow Jane to the kitchen, where she opens a small door. Inside, it's dark. It looks like a black hole.

The stairs look old, like they could fall down at any minute. They creak when we walk down them, too.

At the bottom, Jane grabs the knob on the old, chipped blue door. "Welcome to your bedroom for the night."

The cold air slams into me as soon as we step through.

Jane turns on the light by pulling a string.

Darn it. No way can I get that, it's next to the lightbulb. Maybe I can find something later to stand on if I need to reach it. The smell of the basement and the darkness wrap around me.

Jane smiles. "Perhaps a night down here will make you think twice the next time you want to hurt my daughter."

I doubt it. This lady doesn't know me. If the book game didn't break me in my first foster home, this basement is nothing.

It's huge down here and I didn't know floors could be made out of dirt. It's like a huge mud fort… and the air is definitely colder.

I've got this. This ain't nothin' I've been through more crap than this. I gotta think of it as my special hideout tunnel when I lived with Momma Johnson. My mind wanders back to Patty, the slave girl that was hiding in the underground cave with her doll. If she had to do it, then so can I.

Chapter 6
Just Another Door

"Let's watch how you handle this." Jane flicks the light off with a touch to the cord. "If this light comes on at all tonight, or if you open the door, you'll be down here after school tomorrow, too."

I say nothing because I'm not going to let her know I'm scared. I don't want *any*one to see that. I've faced worse than Jane's dark basement.

The cold, though… This is kinda worse than the darkness. I rub goosebumps on my arms that have suddenly popped up. "Brrr, it's cold," My teeth even chatter in the icy air down here.

Jane restores the light with a click, revealing dust dancing in the beam. "That's not my problem." She narrows her eyes. "Maybe you should have worn pants to school today instead of those flimsy shorts, considering how chilly it is."

In a fit of frustration and anger, I snap at her. "I didn't choose this. *You* took it from my drawer for me to wear."

She stops on the first step, then looks at me, smirking. "I guess I did."

"Jane, can you throw a blanket down for me?"

Jane walks to the string. With a pull, the room is dark. "Nope. You get nothing when you are in the basement for punishment. And how many times do I have to tell you to call me Momma Jane? Maybe you can live down here 'til you do."

Then I'll live down here. Calling her that, will NEVER happen.

I peek past her shadow, scanning the room for clues before she leaves. The outside lamp pole's shining through the small window.

Good. Perhaps that will give me a little light in this dark, damp, and musty place.

Huge, moss-covered stones form the walls, and the ground is packed dirt. There's a small opening in the wall in the corner, barely visible, like an opening to a tunnel or something. I point to it. "What's in there?"

"Stay out of that area—if you don't listen to me and go in there, well, I can't help what'll happen to you."

This woman has put me some place where I can get hurt? That's crazy. She doesn't know that a dark room is not as bad as Derek, Mrs. Dorsey, or even Scott in the last foster home.

"Yeah, well, I'm not afraid of any dark room." I hold my smile and get ready for her to slap my face because that's what other foster mothers did when I sassed back. But... wait. She can't see me.

"Good. You should have no problem sleeping down here, then." She pauses before she pulls the blue door shut. "If you lay hands on my daughter again, you might find this place to be your new bedroom." With a thunderous bang, the door slams.

The musty smell of this place fills my nostrils, a chilling reminder of what tonight will be, with the cold so intense my bones hurt already. My legs shake and knock together as I hug myself.

I shiver when I look at the dark, opening. It's pitch-black. I probably shouldn't go in there, but I don't want to be down here all night being afraid of something. The thought of what's in there is probably worse than what it actually is.

I stand up and take a few steps. Nope. It's not happening. I can't see anything on the ground in front of me except blackness. I don't know where I'm going and what I could run into. Falling down and getting hurt all by myself is a scarier thought than the dark room.

A sudden loud *bang* makes me jump. *Where the heck did that come from?*

I jerk my head—the sudden movement making my neck ache—but

I see that the blue door is shut tight. That's not where the noise came from.

Then… two red eyes glow in the dim light at me. What's down here with me? Does Jane have a crazy dog that she keeps in the basement?

I back up slowly against the stone wall. Could it be a giant rat?

It doesn't move.

The red eyes stay focused on me as I step backward.

I can't look away. I have to be ready to move fast.

Maybe… I should try to be friends with it.

"Hi there, buddy." I try to slow my breathing so I can talk. "Please don't eat me. I don't think I'd taste very good. Also, I'm too skinny to have much meat on my bones."

The thing doesn't budge.

I wonder why. After all, animals love me—even the crazy ones like Thunder before we became friends. I shouldn't be afraid. Maybe this red-eyed thing is just as afraid of me as I am of it.

"Do you live down here all by yourself? That's sad. I promise I won't hurt you. I know what it's like to be all alone like I am now. My mean foster mother has me locked down here, and I can't get out either." I watch, hoping for the thing to move because, if it doesn't and just continues to stare at me, it could pounce at any minute. I creep backward slowly so I don't startle whatever it is.

With the door handle against my back, I recall Jane's words about facing another night in this place if I choose to open it. That's fine with me. If opening the door saves my life, then tomorrow night it is. At least now I know I need the little bear to rest my head on. Plus, I can plan to bring something, like a pencil, for a weapon to fight back. As of right now, I have nothing, not even shoes, because I'm barefoot.

Look away from it, Anna. Maybe the creature's like a dog and staring into its eyes will cause it to become angrier.

I look at the floor. It's strange how they build houses on top of dirt. I hope it is stronger than my mud-pie houses I use to build in my first foster home.

I slowly raise my head.

The red eyes have not moved.

How can the creature stand so still? Maybe *I* need to take the first steps to explore what it is.

I glance up at the little window that lets in a beam of soft light from the streetlamp. It's not bright enough to show me what's in front of me, but, instead, points it's light at the ceiling

I swing my foot back and forth to check if my next step will hit anything.

Nothing.

I creep forward.

Still nothing.

Here I am again, in another foster home, alone in a dark scary room like I was at Georgia's house in the beating room, hiding from Scott. I don't mind being alone in a place that I pick as my hiding spot, but this is not that. What if I have to pee? What if I get hurt? Will Jane even check on me? Does she care if this thing attacks me? What can this thing do to me that Derek, Mrs. Dorsey, Scott, Georgia, or Mrs. Alex hasn't done already. All of them have hurt me. The book game at my first foster home was way scarier than this.

All of a sudden, I feel a little braver. If I can be strong enough to get away from them, I can do this basement.

My body shakes but not as much as before. I take a few steps toward it. I'm not going to sit down here all night and be afraid. I need to find out what it is.

How can this thing just stand there as I walk closer to it?

As I take another step, my leg bangs into something sharp. Ouch! The cold, hard metal beneath my fingertips feels familiar, like the discarded car parts Daddy kept scattered in the yard.

As my eyes adjust to the darkness, I can make out... a furnace! No wonder it made that sound. Too bad it's not heating this room, though.

Glowing red eyes appear from a crack in the metal.

Aha! Those must be little lights helping the furnace run.

Just then, another loud *bang* sounds, and, this time, the red eyes—and the furnace—shut off.

Whoa. I glance around to find that I'm standing in the doorway to the black room. I had no idea I'd walked this far. Jane told me to stay out of there; if I could see, I'd go in it just because she told me not to.

Slowly, I make my way toward the blue door. If I sit on the ground in front of it, I should be able to see anything coming at me. I know the red eyes are the furnace, but who knows who or what is in the other rooms?

Backed against the wall, I sit, head against the cold stone. Ouch. It's too hard and cold to be comfortable, so I rest my head on my pulled-up knees. I have a feeling that falling asleep will not be easy tonight.

Dr. Sharon Zaffarese-Dippold

Dear Jesus, it's me, Anna. I'm in the basement at my new foster home for punching Marlene. I know that wouldn't make you happy, but she hurt me first. Would you be mad at me if I was just defending myself? Would it be okay then? Well... this foster home is not a good one. It seems like there are more bad ones compared to good ones. Maybe you should make sure only good people become foster parents and make these bad ones stop. I wish I could go to a good one because I don't like this place, and I especially don't like this basement. But I won't let them know that. No one is gonna see me afraid. Well, except you, Jesus. Do you think you can sit with me tonight in this dark place? Though I can't see you, it helps me feel better to believe you are with me. Good night, Jesus. Love, Anna.

I wake up freezing, with my teeth chattering like they're driven by a motor. I look at the window and can see it's still dark outside, so it's not morning yet.

Maybe if I rub all of me, my body will warm up and won't hurt from being in this position all night.

I rub my legs, trying to make the goosebumps go away. It works for a few seconds, but that's all.

In gym class, I get hot when we're running around, so maybe I should try jumping jacks and see if that works.

My feet hurt. I move to rub them over and over, trying to make them warm up, but my cold hands aren't helping with that.

How can someone treat a kid like this? I wouldn't even do this to an animal. *C'mon, Anna, stand up. I know it hurts, but do it anyway.*

I can only do four jumping jacks because my legs feel like they're gonna snap in half, they're so stiff. Why does stuff like this keep happening to me? Marlene's the one that should be down here.

I sit back down on the cold dirt. Marlene is so lucky to have a mother who sticks up for her. I don't even know what that feels like anymore. Daddy, in my first home, stuck up for me with Derek. But then I had to leave. Jane's not making Marlene leave. Does that mean she loves her more than Daddy loved me?

I shake my head. That's not true. Daddy loved me.

I hug my knees, but I'm still freezing my butt off. I try pretending I'm sitting next to Daddy's chair that was by the heater in that house. At this moment, I swear I can smell Daddy's cologne. I miss him. He loved me, I know he did. "Dolly wanna help me shave?" he'd ask as he sat me on the sink to watch him. He taught me to dance, too. And… he taught me to love. Thinking about Daddy makes me feel warm inside.

Daddy, Jessica, and Momma Johnson showed me they cared about me. They would never leave me in the basement. I squeeze myself tighter as I think about Daddy's Old Spice that he wore all the time. I could smell it over the oil in the garage. I swear I can smell it now.

I squeeze my knees together to get warm… but it doesn't work. I need to find another way. Maybe I can open the door just a little bit and try to sit on the step. It could be warmer there.

I stand slowly, but when I try to move, my body refuses. It's too cold.

Move it Anna, your legs won't break. You have to find a warm place before you freeze to death.

I try to turn the doorknob, but nothing happens.

It's *locked.* Jane *locked me in.*

All of a sudden, things around me get darker, and my heart races, and I feel like a rat in a trap. Why did she lock me in here?

I breathe fast and feel like I can't stop.

Anna, slow down. Breathe. Slow down. Breathe. Think about Daddy, Curtis or Jesus.

Finally, I start to feel better. This must be how Curtis felt when Derek would lock him in the bathroom at our first foster home. I wonder if he hated that it as much as I hate this.

I lean my head back on my knees. Maybe singing will help me feel better.

Jesus loves me, this I know, for the bible tell me so. Little ones…

I'm startled by the door hitting me in the back.

"Anna, get up. You have to leave for school."

I stand slowly.

Jane pops her head into the room. She doesn't even say, "Good morning," just swirls around and goes back up the steps.

I get to my feet as fast as I can because there's no way I'm gonna give her the chance to lock me in here again. She said I hafta go to school and I'm gonna. At least, there, I have Marie and Mrs. Swing, and no cold, hard floor with a creepy, loud furnace.

My legs hurt with each step, but I don't care. I'm gonna get up to those bright lights in the kitchen.

I almost fall forward, but then, the smell of bacon—and Marlene's nasty face—keep me from doing that because there's no way I'm gonna do that in front of her.

"You're going to school looking like *that*?" she says.

"Marlene, mind your own business," Jane says. "Put your dish in the sink, then head to school."

"Jane. I'm hungry. Can I have some food?" I whisper.

"Sorry, Anna, you can't, or you'll be late for school."

"I'm cold and I don't want to wear shorts to school today. And I want socks because my feet are freezing." I cross my arms and glare at her.

"Don't get fresh with me," she snaps. "Grab a pair of socks out of the dryer and get to school."

"Where's the dryer?" I ask.

Jane takes a gigantic sigh. She points to the small opening off the kitchen. "It's in that room."

How would I know where it is? I haven't been in that room yet.

"Hey, Anna," Jenna says as she runs into the table. "Are you okay? You look as white as a ghost."

"No. I'm freezing. It was cold down there."

Jane doesn't even turn around when I say this—which is surprising because I'd thought for sure she'd yell at me for complaining.

"Hurry up, girls. You don't have time to lollygag—get walking to school."

I run to the dryer, then pull out some socks. Finally, my feet feel warm.

We make it out the door—I'm surprised when Jane hands me lunch. At least I get something to eat today. I might have to eat it on the way to school.

"So, whatcha got going on at school today, Anna?"

"Nothing, except staying away from Marlene. I hate that she's in my class. I wish I could change classes, but I like my teacher."

"I'd hate that, too. I try to stay out of her way, so she'll leave me alone. Make sure not to tell anyone about the basement. Jane tells me if I do, I'll get a belt on top of being down there another night."

Jenna's plan is a good one. For some reason, I'm on the direct path of Marlene and I think it's only going to get worse.

Just Another Door

Then, unexpectedly, it's as if bricks land on both my feet. They begin to hurt and burn like coals in a fire. I stop and bend over to rub them. "Ouch!"

"My feet do that, too, after I've spent the night in the basement." Jenna looks sad right now.

I stop walking and face her. "Why do they do that? They really hurt."

Jenna points to my feet. "A foster mom told me that if your feet get really cold, they hurt when they warm up."

I start to walk. "Yes, they were freezing last night. I just want to think about something else, Jenna, and not school either."

Jenna grabs my hand. Why does she do that? I don't like people touching me.

Just as I'm about to let go of her hand, Marlene bumps into Jenna and knocks her over.

My foster sister slams into the ground and cries out. "Ouch!"

Marlene laughs. "You two in love or something?"

I walk in front of her.

Marlene steps closer to me. Our noses almost touch. "Go ahead, Anna. Hit me. I *dare* you." She taps my nose with her finger.

I lean close to her face. "You know... It looks like someone beat the shit out of you." I lean back, giggling. "If you want to keep all your pretty white teeth, you'll back the hell off."

The smile on Marlene's face disappears as she steps back. "You touch me again, Anna Snow, and you'll spend another night in the basement. That's a perfect place for you, Scumbag." Marlene runs ahead to her friends.

"She really ain't worth the basement, Anna, though you did a good job on her face. Just try to ignore her."

I pull Jenna up from the ground. Ignore her? That ain't easy to do. I can't stand people making fun of me or getting in my face, so I don't know how long I can ignore Marlene.

I have a feeling that I may be spending a lot of time in the basement.

"Good morning, An—" Mrs. Swing stares at me. "Um. Um." She pauses again as another student talks with her.

I take the opportunity to walk to my desk and sit down.

Why did she look at me weird? Does she know that something was wrong and that's why she stopped talking? What could she do to help me?

"Are you okay? You look sick." Marie watches as I pull out my chair.

"I'm okay. It was a rough night in my house." I sit at my desk. I lift my foot onto my chair so I can rub it. It's the only thing that makes it feel better. They really hurt.

"I'm sorry. Was it Marlene?"

"Kinda. But I don't want to talk about Marlene right now." I don't mean to be rude, but I don't want to talk about it anymore.

"No problem, Anna. I get it."

I think it's nice that she's trying to understand, but there's no way she can figure out my life when I can't. No one can answer anything for me. Heck, I don't even know my real birthday or my real mother. It just sucks.

I reach into my desk to look for the material I need to get started for the day. I can barely keep my eyes open, I'm so tired.

"Class, please pull out your reading books and read Chapter 1. There will be a quiz at the end of the period." Everyone sighs except for Marie, of course.

"Goody. I love to read." She claps her hands together so loudly that everyone turns to see her.

"I'm glad you're happy, Marie. I will be calling students up to my desk to go over your grades so far in the class. Anna, can you come up first, please?"

I duck behind the half-wall to sit next to Mrs. Swing.

"Anna," she whispers, "are you okay? Your skin is pale, and you're covered in goosebumps. Are your feet all right? I noticed you're limping."

"My feet hurt bad. My foster sister says it's because my feet were so cold last night and they hurt when they warm up."

"May I see your feet, Anna? Would that be okay?"

What happens if I show her? Jenna said Jane would get mad and put me in the basement again, but what will it hurt to show her my feet? That doesn't mean I'm telling her anything right now.

I peel off my sneakers and socks.

"Wow, your toes are all red and swollen. Yes, this can happen when you get cold and then warm up fast." She reaches down and touches my toes—ew, gross. "Does this hurt?"

"Yes." Why did I tell her that my toes hurt? She's just going to ask more questions. Did I just do something wrong that will make things worse for me at home?

Just Another Door

"Let's check them out later to see if they feel better." She taps my feet lightly. "Do you want to talk about how your feet got so cold?"

What should I do? Maybe if I tell her, she'll understand because she was a foster kid, too. So maybe this happened to her.

"Um... In the foster home, if you get in trouble, the timeout room is in the basement and it's cold down there." I focus on my feet, not on Mrs. Swing. I don't know why I can't look at her when I tell her what happened to me. Maybe she'll think it's my fault because I decked Marlene. *Was* it my fault? Maybe I deserved it.

"How long were you in timeout? You're wearing the same clothes that you had on yesterday, so..."

What do I tell her? If I tell her and she tells Jane, I'll have to spend *another* night in that awful basement. Will it even matter? What can Mrs. Swing do to help me? Why does she care? Maybe it's because she was a foster kid, too. Who better to tell what's going on than someone who lived this horrible life?

"Well, I had to spend the night in the basement because I beat up Marlene yesterday when she pushed me to the ground." I show Mrs. Swing my hands.

She gasps. "Anna, did your foster mother examine your hands? There are tiny rocks under your skin, and they need to be cleaned so they don't get infected." Her finger skims the cuts on my hands.

"I showed her, but Jane didn't care. All she was worried about was Marlene's puffy cheeks where I hit her." I put my head down.

"Well, violence is not the answer."

Of course she'd say this. Adults always do, but they don't care *why* I had to hit her. Maybe Mrs. Swing *doesn't* understand. Maybe being a foster kid was different when she was one.

"But, of course, when you're a foster child, there are times when you *have* to fight to protect yourself. This sounds like one of those times."

What? Did she just agree with me? I think she did. She *does* get it.

"Let's go see the nurse about your hands. We should make sure there's no infection."

I nod, hoping they're not infected. Not that Jane would care if they were. She didn't care that I was cold and in the basement all night by myself, so why would she give a crap about my hands?

"Anna, how long were you in the basement?"

I should tell her—I mean, I'd promised myself I *would* tell her so...

I need to. After all, she gets it. She knows what it's like to be me, so maybe this will help me.

"I was... um... I was in the, um... basement all night." I have to say the last part fast, so I won't chicken out. I've never told something to an adult who might actually believe me.

Mrs. Swing gasps. "Is... is the basement finished? I mean, does it have a floor, carpet, heat?"

Oh, it had a floor. A dirt one... I shake my head. "No heat."

"*What?!*" Mrs. Swing screams out.

"Are you okay back there Mrs. Swing?" Marlene yells.

Great. Just what I need—Marlene getting involved and reporting back to Jane. For sure, I'm going to be sleeping back down there again tonight.

Maybe this wasn't such a good idea to tell my teacher.

Mrs. Swing stands up and looks at the other students. "I'm fine. Keep reading..." She sits back down. "Anna, it was freezing last night, about thirty degrees; what did you have to keep you warm?"

I reply, "Uh... Nothing." Oh, boy. If I am trusting the wrong person, I might end up *living* in the basement.

"When did you go into the basement and when did you get out?" She's mad. I can tell by her scrunched-up face because I've made enough people angry before to know what that looks like.

"When I got home from school and right before I came back."

"Did you eat dinner or breakfast this morning?"

I shake my head. Jane didn't care if I ate. She just wanted to be mean to me because I beat up her precious daughter who hurt me first.

Mrs. Swing takes a deep breath. "Are you still cold?"

I nod. My bones feel like they may be cold for days. But I won't tell Jane that. I don't want her to know that the basement bothers me at all. She wants it to. She wants me to be afraid of it and I won't.

"Okay, let's go to the nurse first to get those hands taken care of. Then we'll get you some warm clothes from the school office and something to eat." She pats my hand. "Thank you for trusting me. I know a bad foster home when I hear one—not all of them are, but you shouldn't be sleeping in a basement in thirty-degree weather in shorts without a blanket. I was lucky and found a nice home when I was twelve, just a few years older than you are now. Maybe you'll find a nice one, too, but this one doesn't sound like it is."

As we stand side-by-side, Mrs. Swing grasps my hand in hers.

In a quick motion, I pull it back, making sure that the kids didn't see it.

Mrs. Swing glances at me and smiles. "Stay here for a second. I'll be right back."

If the kids saw her holding my hand, they'd call me the teacher's pet. I don't need any more names. Does she want to hold my hand because she's trying to help me? Did I hurt her feelings because I pulled my hand back? I hope not. I don't want her to be mad at me.

Class, keep reading. I have to take Anna somewhere, so Ms. Debrah will be in to monitor."

Mrs. Swing leaves me standing behind the half-wall while she leaves the classroom. Marlene points at me and says something to the kids around her and in seconds they laugh.

"Shut up, Marlene," Marie yells in that jerk's direction. "And all of you—"she points to all the kids laughing at whatever Marlene just said—"don't you have anything better to do than go along with her stupid comments?"

I really like Marie. I haven't had a lot of people stand up for me, but now I have Jenna, and Marie, and Mrs. Swing

Just then, Mrs. Swing comes back into the class with a short lady with gray hair.

"Come, Anna, let's get you taken care of."

I follow Mrs. Swing out the door and down the hall. What is going to happen now? Can she help me? Why did I tell her about the basement and Jane? What happens if she tells someone? Can I trust her?

Chapter 7
Spaghetti Fork

"Hello, Mr. Jim, I'd like you to meet Anna Snow." Mrs. Swing points in my direction.

"Well, hello, Anna Snow. What a pretty name for such a tiny little thing. I hope you are liking our school so far?" The principal looks nice enough with his dark curly hair and his beard.

"I am, thanks."

"We need to get Anna's hands checked out by Nurse Faye. Is she around?" Mrs. Swing looks around the office.

"She'll be right back; she needed to check on another student. Go ahead and take Ms. Anna into her office. You and I can talk later."

Mrs. Swing nods. "Sounds good."

Nurse Faye's office is like every school nurse's office I've ever seen. The last time I was in one at my old school, the nurse helped me feel better, so I like this office.

Mrs. Swing digs around in a closet and finds me some sweatpants and a sweatshirt. "Go ahead and pull these sweatpants over your shorts;

you can start warming up now. I'd wait on the sweatshirt until after the nurse checks out your hands." She points to the door. "The restroom's over there. And don't worry, Anna; I'm not going anywhere, so I'll make sure no one disturbs you."

Hmmm, is *she* scared of the bathroom like I am? "Thanks. That makes me feel better."

Mrs. Swing winks. "I thought so. It used to bother me, too."

I turn and walk to the *restroom*. She *does* know what it's like. I thought it was just me being weird. But Mrs. Swing must not like bathrooms either, because she said she'd stand by the door. I wonder if all foster kids don't like that room.

That's a new word for me, and I might start using it since the word *bathroom* makes me get a yucky feeling in my stomach.

And you know what? Since Mrs. Swing is out there and I know she knows that I don't like bathrooms—I mean, restrooms—I don't feel like I need to check the lock like normal.

These pants fit and, boy, they are going to keep my legs warm. My toes aren't hurting as much anymore either, now that I'm warming up.

I open the door—oh, wow, Mrs. Swing hadn't been joking; she's actually guarding the door.

"Oh, Anna, they fit perfectly. And they look warm."

"Thanks, they *are* perfect!"

The lady at the desk with short, blonde hair smiles at me. "Hello, Anna, I'm Nurse Faye. It's nice to meet you. Can I look at your hands?"

"Sure," I'm not *really* sure about this. It seems my hands are always being touched by people. I even got stitches in them once when I was little.

"Come sit on the bed so I can get a better view under this light."

I hop onto the bed, but have to squint. "Wow, that light's really bright."

"I know. Sorry for that, but it helps me see under your skin. If it hurts your eyes, look at Mrs. Swing." Nurse Faye brings my hands close to her face and moves them this way and that. "You're right, Mrs. Swing. There are a few pebbles under her skin. I think it best if we get them out."

"Get them out?" My voice scratches like I ate something sharp. "How do you do that?"

"It might hurt just a little. I'll do my best to be as careful as possible." Nurse Faye gets out a tiny needle from a package like my old foster mom used for sewing—and like they used when I had to go to the hospital to sew up my hands before. "Anna, have you ever had stitches before?"

"Yeah." Twice—after I'd pulled the first round out.

"This won't hurt like that, but it'll probably sting. You need to keep your hand still, okay? Maybe you can just look at Mrs. Swing to take your mind off it."

Mrs. Swing leans close to me. "I'm here, Anna. This will only take a few seconds. We need to remove the rocks to prevent infection."

I nod, biting my lip. Needles make me nervous.

"What's your favorite animal?" Mrs. Swing asks.

I know what she's doing—distracting me. I used to do that with Curtis so he wouldn't cry and get into trouble at our first foster house. When the boys were trying to scare him, I would make a funny face to get him to laugh instead. It always worked. "Horses. They're my favorite animal—ouch!"

"I'm sorry, Anna. Almost done," says Nurse Faye.

Boy, she wasn't kidding when she said it would sting. This hurts almost as bad as those stitches.

"Did you ever have any horses in other foster homes?" Mrs. Swing asks.

I blow out a breath; I *do* need to focus on her so I don't yank my hand from Nurse Faye. "In one of them, I became friends with a crazy horse in the barn next door—ouch."

Mrs. Swing laughs. "A crazy horse, huh?"

"Yeah, he didn't like anyone else but me." For a second, the needle in my hand is nothing compared to the pain of losing Thunder. I miss him.

"All done. I'll grab some peroxide to make sure the area is clean."

I check my hand; there's some blood, but the little stones are gone. Ya know, 'bout the only good thing about being so cold last night was that I forgot my hands were hurting.

Nurse Faye returns with a brown bottle. She makes a motion for me to join her at the sink. "Don't worry, Anna. This won't hurt at all. It will actually make bubbles on your hand. Let's find out how many bubbles your skin makes."

She's right. The liquid makes my hands bubble up, and it doesn't hurt at all.

With a smile, Nurse Faye covers the cuts with a brightly colored bandage. "You didn't move your hands once—good girl. Now, you're all set. These should heal nicely."

"Thank you, Nurse Faye," says Mrs. Swing. "We're going to head to the cafeteria so we can find Anna something to eat. She's a hungry girl this morning."

Mrs. Swing and Nurse Faye kinda stare at each other like they're reading each other's minds or something.

As if on cue, my stomach growls so loud it echoes in the nurse's office. We all laugh.

"I think that is a good idea, Mrs. Swing."

My teacher gets me my favorite foods—a peanut butter-and-jelly sandwich, some milk, and a few chocolate chip cookies.

She has a cookie, too, when she sits down with me. Right before she takes another bite, she asks, "Anna, is anything bad happening to you at your foster home?"

Other than having to freeze in the basement? I'm not sure how to answer her.

"Is someone being mean to you there?"

That's easier to answer. "Marlene."

"What does Marlene do to you?"

"The same thing she does in class. She likes to make fun of me and get me going." I clear my throat. "I don't like her at all."

"Sometimes, kids can be mean."

This isn't news to me; they seem to follow me from one foster home to another.

Mrs. Swing sets her cookie down. "Anyone else in the home?"

I take another bite of my sandwich because I'm too hungry to stop to talk.

"Does Jane or Roger... hit you?"

"Nope."

"Do they scream at you a lot?"

"Not really, just when I punch Marlene in the face. I've only been there two days."

Mrs. Swing giggles, then puts a hand over her mouth. "Were you afraid in the basement?"

"I wasn't really, except for the red eyes. But, after a while, I found out they belonged to the furnace."

"That sounds scary." She pats my hand.

"It was at first."

"Could you leave the basement if you wanted to?" Mrs. Swing takes a bite of her cookie.

"Nope. The door was locked." I take a swig of milk. I'm not a fan, but when I drink out of the carton, I can't see my teacher. I think she's trying to help by asking questions, but I'm afraid of getting in trouble for answering them.

"How did you know the door was locked?"

"Because I tried to open it to see if the steps would be warmer than where I was sitting. But it was locked."

"Where you scared then?"

I shrug. "A little, I guess. I didn't like it."

"I bet you didn't. I wouldn't have liked it either." She crosses her eyes, making me giggle. "Well, since our bellies are both full on cookies, are we ready to head back to class? And let's get this sweatshirt on you so you can be warm."

We walk back. I don't mind that I'm gonna see Marlene because my stomach's full, my hands are better, and my feet are warm.

I walk into the classroom and Marlene—of course—just *has* to say something mean. "What the heck? Where did *Dirty* get those clothes?"

"Enough, Marlene—unless you *want* to sit in the hallway again and have me call your mother?" Mrs. Swing points to the door.

Marlene shuts up for once. But what my teacher doesn't know is that her mother wouldn't do anything to punish her, anyway.

"Hey, Anna." Marie smiles at me as I pass her seat to take mine. "I like the sweatsuit."

"Thanks." I remember at my old school when Sharon said she liked the clothes the school gave me. Marie just did the same. It feels good when people say nice things. I don't get that very often. Not from school or my foster homes.

Before long, we are back at the foster home.

Jane meets us at the door. "Do you have any—" She looks me up and down. "Where did you get those clothes?"

"My teacher because I was cold." Jenna's fidgeting, but I'm not afraid of Jane. If I could stand up to Mrs. Dorsey, who beat the crap out of me for it, I can stand up to Jane—and I'm going to. "She gave me warm clothes because you wouldn't. I told you I was cold, and you didn't listen." Glaring, I cross my arms. I *will* be strong.

Jane squints at me and her mouth looks like she's got too many words that want to come out, so she takes a few seconds before actually saying anything. "Jenna, go to your room. I need a moment with your foster sister."

Just Another Door

Jenna glances at me. Poor kid is scared. But I'm not. I didn't do anything wrong.

Jane stares at me like we're in a staring contest.

She has no idea how good I am at this game—and I have no plans to lose this one.

"So…" She taps her foot. "You went crying to your teacher, all snot-nosed and shivering, because you were cold, huh?"

"Yup. I did."

"What else did you tell them?"

"Nothing. Can I go now, please? My legs hurt just standing on this porch." I don't care about lying to her since I don't like her, anyway. I'll explain it to Jesus later.

"Get out of my sight, you *poor wittle girl*."

She thinks words will hurt me? Ha.

"Just remember *why* I punished you, and keep your hands off my daughter."

Trust me, I don't want to be anywhere near Marlene so that's not gonna be a problem. Unless, of course, Marlene gets in my business again. Then, I'll get in hers.

I hurry to my room to get away from this mean woman, climb up onto my bed and hug my stuffed friends.

"Anna, are you sleeping in the room with me tonight?" Jenna asks.

"Yes, I am." Looking down from my bed, I notice her all tucked into her blankets. "Are you okay? Your voice sounds funny."

A tear slides down her cheek. "Anna, can I tell you something?"

"Of course! We're SnowStorm. You can tell me anything and I'll never tell anyone anything you tell me." I stick out my pinky finger and wait for her to pinky-swear.

She doesn't. She just lies there as another tear rolls down her face.

"What's the matter? What happened?"

Jenna brushes the tears away. "Last night… when you weren't in here…" She clears her throat. "Um… Roger came in in the middle of the night and… woke me up."

Oh, no. Please don't let Roger have done to Jenna what Derek did to me. "What happened, Jenna? What did Roger do to you?" My ears and face are heating like they're on fire.

Jenna starts to sob.

I jump off my bed and get into hers. "What did he do, Jenna?"

"He... um... He..." She takes a big breath. "He... rubbed me... here." She points to the place where I know all too well—her girl parts.

Oh, no. I'm so sad for her. "Did he... did he do anything else to you?" I don't want to know, but maybe Jenna wants to tell me. I wish I'd had a foster sister that I could've told what was happening to me with Derek, Mrs. Dorsey, and Scott, so I'll be here for her.

"He said that I'm becoming his big, special girl, and he wants to get me ready for that kind of relationship. He, um, said that big girls do special things with their fathers. He asked me if I wanted a daddy."

I clench my fists. That's what my old foster mother, Sue, had told me when she'd wanted to have *girl time* when she'd asked me to do things with her because *that's what girls do with their mother*. She lied to me, just like Roger's lying to Jenna now.

I'm going to blow fire at any minute and my stomach aches because Jenna's story reminds me of some bad times. "Did he do anything else?" *Please, Jesus, don't let him have done anything else to her.* "I'm here and you can tell me anything. I promise I won't tell anyone."

Jenna puts her head on my shoulder and wraps her arms around my waist. "He said he needed to teach me how to kiss like the special girl I am. He put his tongue in my mouth." Jenna shakes her head into my shoulder. "It was so gross, Anna. I wanted to bite his tongue off."

"Maybe you should have." We both crack up at that. "But, seriously, Jenna, if I ever have to sleep in the basement again, I'll show you how to barricade the door with that chair over there. If he tries to push it open, the chair will stop him or make too much noise for him to get in. Trust me, he won't want to wake up Jane if he's trying to sneak into our room."

Jenna sits up quickly. "Can you show me now? I want to know how to do it now, in case you're not here."

"Okay." I get up, grab the chair, then show her how to tilt it under the doorknob. "See?"

Jenna smiles for the first time since I got back to the room. "Can I see how it works, Anna? You stand outside the door and try to get in."

"Okay." I go out of the room and wait for her to tell me it's ready. I turn the knob and push.

The door doesn't budge.

I push harder.

Nothing.

"Yay, Anna! It works! It really works!"

I knew that already because I'd had to use the chair to protect myself from my foster brothers in the last home. Every girl should have one in their room.

I go back into the room and we sit on the floor together. "Are you okay, Jenna?"

She nods. "But I'm afraid. I don't want Roger to touch me again. I don't like it, it didn't feel good. And I never, ever want to kiss him again."

"Well, I'll be in here with you, so he won't bother you, and, like I said, if I have to sleep in the basement, you can set the chair up to keep him out."

"Thank you, Anna, for helping me with this."

"Well, thank you, too—for suggesting I take your bear. I know why you wanted me to have it, so, next time, I'll take it with me."

"I hope you won't have to." Jenna's eyes get watery again.

I don't want her to cry, but I'm pretty sure I'll be in that basement again. "Hey, you know what?"

"What?"

"Since we're sisters now, let's have a special handshake that no one else knows but us."

"Oh, I like that idea." Jenna's smiling again, thank goodness. "I've always wanted a sister, Anna. I don't like not having a family and being all alone."

"Me, too, Jenna…"

Our bedroom door flies open, and Barry comes running in. "Can I play?"

"No, Barry, it's just Anna and me. Why don't you go play with your toys?"

Barry puts his head down and pouts.

He reminds me of Curtis, especially that hanging-his-head thing, and I could never stand when my brother was sad. "Hey, Barry, come here and let me show you something."

Jenna scrunches her face at me, but I don't want to make anyone sad if they don't deserve it. "I'm going to teach you how to play rock, paper, scissors."

"Cool!" Barry gets a big smile and plops on the floor in front of me.

It only takes two rounds for him to get the hang of it, but then he's done. "Thanks, Anna, but I want to go play with my toys now." He sprints out of our bedroom door.

I guess he just didn't want to be alone. But it's weird that this is the first time he's actually come to talk to us besides at dinner. He hasn't been around for the last few days.

"He goes to visit his real grandmother for a week at a time sometimes," Jenna says.

"Huh? Why? I thought the Tarts were adopting him,"

"They are, but he still gets to visit his real grandmother, too."

"I wish I had a real grandmother."

"Me, too, Anna."

"You don't have anyone from your real family to visit you either?" I whisper.

"Nope. No one.

I guess you and me are alike in that way, too, but at least we have each other right now."

She's so right. But I've had friends before and then lost them; I hope I don't lose Jenna. "It is, and I promise to be the best friend ever, Jenna. And I promise to do whatever I can to keep Roger away from you."

Jenna leans over and gives me a hug.

I want to keep hugging her for a long time.

"Both of you get down here for dinner!"

Of *course* Jane has to ruin it. Sometimes, hugs are more important than food.

But since I don't want to sleep in the basement again—especially now that I know how much Jenna needs me—I get off the floor. "Come on, let's go. I'm hungry."

"Me, too." Jenna giggles.

I'd rather hear that than see her cry—which is why I'm not going to tell her what Derek did to me. Her story reminds me of that, but how can I protect her from Roger—a grownup—when I'm just a kid couldn't protect myself from Derek—another kid?

We have spaghetti for dinner, and I dig in, not bothering to talk to anyone. I'm not gonna give Jane the chance to starve me if I can help it.

Of course, Marlene is the center of attention at the table, both Jane and Roger talking about how proud they are of her. Even Barry says that he likes having her as his big sister.

Marlene blows him a kiss.

Seriously gross.

Just Another Door

To me, though, Marlene sticks out her tongue.

Like that hurts my feelings. Ha! But I do return the favor with a spaghetti-filled mouth.

"Mommmmmm, tell Anna to keep her mouth closed when she has food in it. Did you see her stick her tongue out at me? I don't know if I can eat my food now."

"Nuh uh. Marlene stuck her tongue out at me first. I just did the same with a little spaghetti." I can't help it smiling a little at the end—serves Marlene right, the lying whiner.

Jane's face turns red.

Good! I don't care if she's mad. I hate this woman, and she's a horrible foster mother.

Jenna reaches over and taps my leg as Roger walks into the room and grabs the chair next to her.

"Roger, why are you sitting there? I left the seat open for you down here by me?" Jane sounds frustrated.

"That's okay, honey. I wanted to sit here today," he replies with a smile.

After a few minutes of eating my spaghetti, Jenna grabs my leg under the table.

I look at her. She's not eating—or even moving, just staring at her plate.

She squeezes my leg. Hard.

"Ouch!" I can't stop myself from saying it, but I kinda know I shouldn't have.

Everyone stops eating and stares at me.

"Uh... Sorry. I, uh... I think something bit me."

"Don't be so dramatic, Anna," Jane snaps back.

I fake an itch to bend over so I can see what's going on with Jenna.

And then I completely understand.

Roger's sneaky hand is making its way up Jenna's leg, heading toward her girl parts under the table!

I promised to protect her and I will. "Hey, Jenna, can I change places with you? I don't want to sit across from Marlene because I might make her mad."

Marlene cackles—and I don't care. I have bigger things to worry about. Plus, if she—and Jane—think it's because of this, they won't say I can't move.

"Good idea, Scumbag. I'm glad you finally figured out that I don't want to be around you."

Jenna hops up fast, and we trade places.

"Hey, Roger, can you move your chair over a little so I can sit down?" I put on my biggest smile and use my sweetest voice." If he puts his hand on my leg, I will stab him with the fork, and I won't care.

I pick up the fork and examine it, just like the school nurse did with my hand. "This fork looks like the pitchforks that used to be in the barn with my horse, Thunder, a few foster homes ago. Did you know that you can use these to protect yourself if you have to?"

The entire table stops talking and they all watch me twirl the fork in the air. I'm sure I sound crazy, but I don't care. I want Roger to understand what I'll do with it if he even *thinks* of touching me.

He just stares at me.

I'm pretty sure he got the message.

"Anna sounds like a serial killer, Mother. Do we have a killer living in our house?" Marlene looks scared and scoots her chair back. She should be an actress.

"Anna, that's enough of the crazy talk. Use the fork for what it's supposed to be used for and stop messing around!" Jane yells.

I glare at Roger as I keep the fork in the air. Then, still glaring at him, I scoop up a bite of spaghetti.

For a second, Roger's face turns into Derek's.

I'm sitting next to Derek… *and I take the fork and slam it into his hands on the table. Derek screams. That doesn't stop me—I yank the fork out of his bleeding hands, then stab it into one of his legs, and then the other. He keeps screaming, but I don't care. He hurt me, so I'm going to hurt him. Then—*

The doorbell chimes, and Derek's gone, there is no fork in Derek's hand or blood, and Roger is back to sitting at the table.

"Can you get the door, Roger, while I take off my apron and make myself presentable?"

As Roger walks out of the dining room, Jane walks to the sink to hang up her apron.

Jenna leans over and whispers, "Thank you, Anna."

"I got you." I squeeze her hand under the table.

Roger is gone for a bit, but then he walks back and—*Mrs. Alex* is walking through the doorway right behind him.

Chapter 8
Mrs. Swing

Mrs. Alex's red lipstick is the same bright color as it always is, no matter when I see her.

"Hello, Anna." She stands next to the table, glaring at me.

What'd I do now? I haven't been here long to do anything bad enough for her to show up. Of course, that isn't going to stop her. Mrs. Alex is evil. "Uh, hi, Mrs. Alex?"

"Well, hello, Mrs. Alex. This is a pleasant surprise. We didn't know you were coming. What can we do for you?" Jane sounds nice. Gross, she's faking.

My caseworker clears her throat. "I apologize for dropping in, but some information has come to light. I need to speak with the both of you."

"Sure thing, Mrs. Alex. Let's head up to our bedroom so the kids can't hear."

Jane sounds so nice talking to her, it makes me sick. All the bad foster parents know how to sound so perfect. That's why no one ever believes me when I tell them the awful things those *such sweet people* do to me.

When the three of them disappear upstairs, I whisper in Jenna's ear. "Let's go sit on the step so we can talk."

Jenna nods and gets up when I do.

"Where do you think you're going?" Marlene asks like I'm committing the biggest sin known to mankind.

"None of your business. You're not my boss." My chair cracks loudly as I hit the table leg.

"Be careful with that chair. Mom will be mad if you ding it up."

"Your mother will be mad no matter what I do, so be quiet and leave me alone."

"Mom told us all to sit here." Marlene acts like she's in charge.

As if I care. "You're a liar. I didn't hear her say that." I grab Jenna's hand. "Let's go."

We head outside and sit on the bottom step.

"What's going on, Anna?"

"I think my caseworker is here to take me to a new foster home."

"Why?" Jenna's eyes start to fill up again.

I can't blame her. "I don't know, really, but the only time I ever see her is when she's taking me someplace new."

"I don't want you to leave."

"Me either." Wait, *what*? I hate Jane and Marlene, and Roger is... Roger. I shouldn't want to stay here, but... there's Jenna.

"Anna, please don't leave me here with Roger. I'm afraid of him." She wraps her arms around my waist, reminding me of when Curtis used to do that. "Can you ask your caseworker if I can go with you? Please, *please* don't leave me here."

This is the *only* reason I want to stay—to have a foster sister who wants me. Being alone is scary, so having someone who understands and likes you, feels safer—if I could ever describe foster care with that word...

"Let's do our handshake together so we don't think about it." I'm hoping this helps Jenna—heck, I'm hoping it helps *me* because I really don't want to think about why Mrs. Alex is here. I don't want to leave Jenna or Marie or Mrs. Swing.

Jane stomps down the porch steps to us, her face all red. "Anna, Mrs. Alex would like to talk to you. Follow me."

Entering the room, I see Roger sitting on the bed, Mrs. Alex at the desk, and Jane moves to stand in front of me.

"Anna, it looks like we're in a bit of a mess." Mrs. Alex glances at Roger and Jane. "It seems you may be telling stories again."

"What?!" I yell. "Telling stories about what?"

"I received a hotline call from the school today. Supposedly, you told them you are being abused by Jane and Roger?"

"What's a hotline call? What's abuse? I didn't do it since I don't even know what those words mean."

Jane and Roger are talking now, but it's muffled to me—and I don't care anyway. All I care about now is someone I trusted has just caused more problems for me.

"Do you agree, Anna?" Jane asks.

I don't want to talk to her. "I guess," I mumble.

"See, Mrs. Alex? I told you it was a lie. Anna didn't spend the night in the basement."

"Wait!" I jump into the conversation. "That's not true. I *did* have to spend the night in the basement because I punched Marlene in the face."

Mrs. Alex shakes her finger in my direction. "Anna, you can't *do* that. You can*not* be punching kids in the face. That will get you moved from a home faster than anything else."

I cross my arms. "I don't care, Mrs. Alex. It happened because she's mean to me. Why don't you tell the foster parents—" I point to Jane and Roger—"not to be mean to us kids?"

"Anna, I think you may be lying again. I've known these people for a long time, and I find it hard to believe they would put you in that cold, dark basement. I went and saw it for myself."

"You're the liar, not me. Ask the other kids. Ask Jenna." Crap. I shouldn't have brought her into this. "Never mind. You never believe anything I say." I can't *imagine* what Mrs. Alex would say if I tell her what I saw under the table just now. "Can I go now?" I head out of the bedroom, feeling like there's a ton of bricks on my shoulders.

What's wrong with Mrs. Alex? Why doesn't she ever believe me about anything? I've never lied to her. Mrs. Dorsey told her I was lying when she'd pulverized me, and Jane's lying now.

"Anna, come back here."

I ignore Mrs. Alex and continue through the kitchen to head up to my bedroom.

Jenna jumps out of her bed to meet me. "Are you okay? Are you moving?"

I want to push Jenna away because I'm so mad right now, but I don't because this isn't her fault. "Nope. I'm not going anywhere. My caseworker didn't believe me about the basement." I climb onto my bunk and squeeze Teddy and Raggedy.

"How did she hear about the basement?" Jenna stands on her bed so her head is resting on mine.

"I don't know."

But, yeah, I do. I just don't want to talk about it. Mrs. Swing is the only person I spoke to, so I know it was her that told on me. She knows what it's like to be a foster kid, yet she just *had to* go and call Mrs. Alex. I'll never understand why. "I'd like to be alone."

"Okay, Anna." She slides off the bed.

I allow my tears to crawl down my face. The one person I've met so far that I thought I could tell everything to…

I guess I was wrong.

"Anna, wake up."

Jenna wakes me by shoving her bear in my face. "Take this. Momma Jane's on her way up here to get you, and she said that you're spending the night in the basement again for telling on them. She said she was going to show you *and* me what happens when we tell people anything about their family. Take my bear. Tuck it in your pants."

I slide the bear across the bed. "What's that?" I point to the glow coming from the bear.

"It's a pillow *and* a little light!" She grins. "See why it's great for that dark, creepy place? It has a built-in light, and the bear is small enough to fit in your pocket."

"Great idea, Jenna." I jump off the bed, then grab a pencil to put in one of my sweatpants pockets—then I remember, Roger. "Don't forget to block the door tonight with the chair. And scream if he comes into our room. Let Jane see what her precious husband is really like."

"I will. I will." My foster sister's face shows how afraid she is.

"Whatever you do, don't forget the chair, Jenna." I hug her.

Jane bursts into the room. "Get away from her and come with me right now." Her eyebrows look like one giant one. She's pissed. "You are going to spend another night in the basement, young lady. Maybe *that* will stop you from telling people what happens in this house."

I glare at her and cross my arms. "It won't." Though, actually, she *is* right; I'm not going to tell anyone again.

"If it wasn't for the timing right now, we'd be moving your ass out of this house."

"Good. I'd be fine with that." I'm not afraid to show her how mad I am.

"Anna, no, please don't leave! Please don't move her, Momma Jane."

I hate to see Jenna begging this witch for anything.

"Mind your own business, Jenna. This is not about you. We appreciate that you keep our family business private." She glares at me. "Are you trying to get our Marlene taken from us? Do you not want Barry adopted by a family so he'll have to spend his life in foster care like you? Would you like us in jail and Marlene in foster care? Huh?"

I shrug. "I don't care. Maybe Marlene would stop being so mean."

Jane grabs my arm.

I yank it away and jump back. "Get your hands off me!"

Roger runs into the room, out of breath. "Jane." Roger bends over, trying to catch his breath. He looks like he's going to die.

If only...

He stands up. "Jane, take your hands off her. Because of the conversation we just had with the social worker, she may come back to check on Anna. Plus, the school will be keeping an eye on her as well. Just take her to the basement like we talked about. That's punishment enough." He looks at me, frowning.

If only I had the spaghetti fork... "

"Get moving, Anna." Jane can barely get the words out and I see her fingers twitch.

She wants to grab me so bad... At least, even if Mrs. Swing told on me, Jane and Roger are worried enough to not hurt me. That's something.

I twirl around to Jenna before I go, mouthing, "Lock the door tonight."

She nods.

Jane, Roger, and I create a train going down the stairs into the basement.

At least I'm aware of what's down there now. I can't believe Jane didn't ask me what I had in my pants. She can't be *that* dumb.

"You know the rules, but I'll say them again. If you come upstairs or open this door..." she taps, it... "you'll spend tomorrow night down here as well." She smirks. "Maybe *this* will teach you to keep your mouth shut."

Dr. Sharon Zaffarese-Dippold

I glare at her and shake my head.

Her nostrils flare like a bull. "Good, then you'll visit this place a lot."

The old wooden door rattles when she slams it shut. To me, it's just another door and I'm not going to be afraid. I've seen so many doors in my life that take me to places and people I don't know. This place is not that. I know what to expect and now I can explore more of it with my bear light. This will be an adventure.

I sit down, hitting the ground a little harder than I'd planned. While rubbing my sore butt, I feel the damp soil clinging to my clothes. This time, I'm wearing thick, warm socks, comfortable sweatpants, and a soft sweatshirt. At least I'll be warmer this time.

Still… this sucks.

I bury my face in my knees, letting my tears fall. I'm not sad because I'm in the basement; Jane's anger doesn't bother me. Mrs. Alex being here didn't make me sad, either. It's just that… It's…. because…

Why does this happen to me? Why'd Mrs. Swing have to tell? Why was she the *one* grown up I thought I could trust, but then she does this…?

I guess I shouldn't have counted on her. So what that she was a foster kid and knows what it's like? She doesn't love me, so why would she protect me? Even Daddy—who said he loved me and acted like it most times—called Mrs. Alex and got me taken out of my very first foster home; the one where I didn't even know I was a foster kid until just before I left. I mean, sure, he was protecting me from Derek, but why did *I* have to leave and not Derek? Derek was the one who did bad things. Like here—Jane is the one doing bad things. Roger, too. Why can't *they* be made to leave?

Stop crying like a baby. It's not going to help you. Just knock it off.

The furnace bangs on. Now that I know what it is, it's actually more comforting than scary.

"Hello, Furnace. Thank you for shining your red eyes so I can have more light."

I pull the teddy bear out of my pocket and turn on its night light. This will work perfectly to check out that room in the corner.

I use the light to get there without banging into anything, then duck down to head through that doorway.

I shine the light on the floor, so I don't fall into a hole or trip over something. I reach the middle of the room. There's nothing in it so far.

Just Another Door

Then I see a small crack of light over by the wall. I got here while it was still light, so it wasn't dark.

I head toward it and, after a few more steps, I see cement stairs.

"Ow." Something just dug into my head. Rubbing my scalp, I feel something pointy above me. With the bear's belly light, I spot two big metal doors with a small rusty nail sticking out. That must be what poked me. That's okay, though, because *woohoo!* I just found a way out.

My heart races with the excitement for this adventure. I might as well have some fun if I'm stuck down here. A smile forms across my face. I love adventures.

Bending down, I leave the bear on the stairs because I'm going to need both of my hands to open this huge thing. No matter what, I'm going to get outta here.

A groan escapes my lips. I push. *C'mon you darn door*.

Ouch. My back is killing me, but I can't quit.

I grunt loudly. Nothing's happening and the doors are not moving. I have to come up with a different plan. At this rate, I'll be here all night.

I step back and look.

There are two doors, but I need to push on just one of them. I can lift one, right?

You got this, Anna. Get out of here. You got this.

Okay, here we go. One jump, one push, and it opens!

Yay! I did it.

Sunlight blasts me in the face. I'm outside next to the flower bushes, breathing in their sweet smell.

Quietly and carefully, I close the door, hoping to avoid any attention, then I sneak around the house to see if anyone's outside. There are windows all over the house, so if I run into the woods, they might see me. Instead, I look around to see if I can get out of my bedroom window at night in case Roger tries to come in.

Hmmm, I look at the house—wait. There's an old wooden ladder by the shed. I could move that to the window, and, since our room is at the back of the house, no one will see it.

I'll do that when I come back from the woods, because that's where I'm headed first. They'll never find me in there.

Noticing a car parked at the end of the driveway, I make that my first hiding target. I run to it, then duck behind the trunk end.

No one comes out of the house.

Dr. Sharon Zaffarese-Dippold

Phew. I did it. I'm closer to the woods now.

I have to get to those woods because if Jane finds me out of the basement, it'll be my new bedroom for sure.

I sprint, my breath catching in my throat, until I'm surrounded by towering trees that block out the sun. There's no way Roger or Jane will see me here.

A giant oak tree is low enough for me to climb, so I scramble from one branch to another. Before long, I'm high in the tree, the rough bark digging into my thighs as I sit on a sturdy branch and swing my legs. I love the smell of the forest. I have the perfect view of the dining room window and can see everyone walking around. Roger's hugging Jane. Then he kisses her. *Yuck!* It makes me think of what he did to Jenna. Someone should cut his tongue out if he wants to use it on little girls.

Wow, what a view! I can see everything. I notice a little tree house, kinda hidden down by the creek. That needs to be checked out. It looks cool.

The tree limb wobbles a little, creaking under my weight as I carefully make my way back to the trunk to climb down. I only have a few hours of daylight left. I definitely don't want to be caught in the woods at night; the sounds alone would freak me out.

My sweatshirt catches on a branch while I leave the tree. Pulling it tears a little as I get loose. I'll have to hide this from Jane tomorrow because she might ask where it came from. I could just tell her I got attacked in the basement—though she wouldn't even care. My guess is that she won't even ask.

With a quick push off the limb, I jump and land on the leaves. I'm happy I didn't take my shoes off after school. That was good thinking on my part. I better keep them on going forward, just in case Jane locks me up for the night again.

I run down the hill to the tree house. It looks really old, but that's not gonna stop me from climbing the rickety ladder.

This is awesome. It's too far from the house to belong to Roger and Jane.

I look around and see letters carved into the wood. *SC loves SB.* I trace the letters with my finger. Hmmm... I'm gonna put mine here, too.

I don't see anything I can use, but I have the pencil in my pocket. I try that, but, darn it, it breaks.

Oh well. The next time I come, I'll bring a sharp rock so my name can be in this fort forever, no matter where I move to.

I take a seat in a corner and lean my head back against the wood, feeling its rough texture as I close my eyes. The cheerful chirping of birds outside the window causes me to yawn.

Maybe I'll spend the night here, where the air is fresh, rather than in that damp, creepy basement. No one would find me. But... it might be chilly tonight. The cellar's gotta be warmer than this tree house.

I get up and stretch, smiling as my fingers brush some leaves. Jane thinks she's hurting me, but she totally helped me find a new place to hide.

I need to head back since the sun is going down. I'm brave, but walking in the woods at nighttime is not something I want to do. Too bad I can't be sure that I'd wake up before school, or I'd stay out here. Well, that and the cold.

Still... It would be nice.

Closing my eyes, I listen to the birds. I wish I could fly away with them and be anywhere but in my horrible life. I wonder if I will join them when I die. I could fly with them and... I could see Jesus, too.

Slowly, I stand back up and walk to the edge of the tree house. I look down. All I have to do is jump, and this world is all over. I won't have to deal with mean kids or nasty grownups. I won't have to go to new foster homes anymore. This would be the perfect way out of my life. Why should I have to live this way when other kids don't? A tear slides down my cheek.

I hate my life. I hate me. I hate being a foster kid. I hate living.

Boy, that seems a long way down, Anna. Are you sure you want to jump? The voice in my head tries to talk me out of dying today.

I step closer to the edge with half of my feet hanging over. I close my eyes.

I'm going to jump.

Lean forward and push. It will be over in a second and no one can hurt you ever again.

I stand with closed eyes as my toes feel nothing beneath them. The only thing holding me to this awful life is the back of my feet.

Push Anna and it's all over. Just push.

STOP! a voice in my head screams.

It sounds like... Daddy.

Who will watch over Jenna? Roger will have her all to himself. My ears get hot at the thought. No way I'll do that to her. I promised her I'd protect her.

I step back. I won't break my promise.

Maybe visiting Jesus tonight is not such a good idea. If I jump, then all those mean people win. I'll *let* them win. I know people are hurting me, but why should *I* hurt me, too? I'm like Jenna—and if I'm going to protect and fight for her, shouldn't I do that for myself? I'll show all these mean people that they can't get to me. That I'm stronger than them. That... That... I deserve to live, too.

Tears stream down my face. Pressure builds up in my belly and I sob. I can live, too. I can fight for me. Someday, I will be happy.

Someday. I'll fight for that. When I'm a grownup, I'm going to change foster care. I'm going to help other foster kids by telling them we are not garbage. I'll make foster care stop moving us kids with garbage bags. Yup. I'm going to do that. But I have to live to do it, so, no matter what, I can't die.

As soon as my feet hit the ground after climbing down from the tree house, a low, rumbling of leaves fills the air, immediately grabbing my attention. "I hope you're not a wild animal," I announce to whatever's coming my way.

A kitten with dirty paws and soft meows comes out of the low bushes.

I bend down to pet him. "Hey, pretty baby. What's your name?"

He lets out a soft meow and rubs his furry body against my leg.

"Boy, you look skinny. I'll try to bring you some food tomorrow."

With my new friend beside me, I enjoy the smell of the woods as I sit on a sturdy rock.

A sad thought hits me. If I would have jumped, I could've landed on this tiny thing and killed it. That would be awful. And, if I wasn't here, I wouldn't be sitting here with this cute little thing and petting it. If I wasn't here...I'd miss so much.

I jump up and gather leaves while holding the kitty with my other hand. "I'll make a bed for you so you can be warm at night." If I wasn't here, this kitty would have no bed to stay warm. I'm not ever going to think about killing myself again. Instead, I'm going to show all the adults who hurt me that I'm strong. And when I'm grown up, I'll help kids like me, so they don't want to kill themselves either. Why should we let foster care kill us when we can grow up and fight against it?

Before I realize it, the sunlight fades, the air grows cooler, and long shadows stretch across the ground. Time to go.

"'Bye, Kitty. I made a bed for you out of leaves." I place the kitten on the pile. "If you sleep in this tonight, you can stay warm. And then I'll be back tomorrow with some food." I hate leaving this little baby out here, but what else can I do? There's no way I can suddenly have a kitten in the basement—Jane will know I snuck out. And I don't even know if she likes kittens and would let me have one. She probably won't because she's such a nasty person.

I really miss Daddy. At least, at that house, I had Mama Cat.

Or course, I also had Derek…

And now I have Roger. Well, *Jenna* has Roger, and that's just as bad.

And now I have to go back to that house. Ugh.

I reach the edge of the forest, then check if anyone's outside or looking out. The last thing I need is for someone to see me and get in even *more* trouble.

Thankfully, it's safe, so I run back. Now, to get that ladder near my window because I really don't want to get sent to the basement just so I can see the kitten again.

The ladder's heavy, but I'm stronger than I look. Jane will never think I moved it if she even sees it.

She's also never gonna think I snuck out of the basement because when I open the door to go back inside, it's *really* heavy. No way she's gonna think I moved it—'cause I barely can. But I have to, so I don't get in more trouble.

I slide under the door, then close it quietly so no one hears. Using the light from the bear, I find my way back to my sitting spot for the night.

Jenna's right—the bear's a comfy pillow. And since the red eyes don't scare me anymore, this isn't too bad, especially after my outside adventure. It almost makes staying down here worth it. "'Nighty-night, Furnace."

"Hello, Jesus. I'm back in the basement again—this time for trying to tell someone what actually happened. A lot of good it did me. But you know already what happened because you can see everything. Thanks for helping me find a new hiding place. It's great. And thanks for my new kitten, friend. Well, I'm tired, Jesus, so I'm going to sleep now.

I wake up a couple of times in the night because I'm so cold. *And* because I'm excited about my discovery and can't wait to show Jenna. She needs a hiding place, too, so she can be safe.

The sunshine wakes me up the next morning before Jane can. I stand, brushing off my clothes to make sure I have no trace of my adventure from last night on me.

I'm glad I'm up before she is, so she'll see that I wasn't afraid down here. That her plan to punish me didn't work at all.

Jane finally opens the door. "Come on, Anna. Get upstairs and change your clothes. I'll wash them and you can return them to school tomorrow. Oh, and here's a banana. I can't let you go to school hungry."

"Good morning, Jane. I actually had a really good sleep."

I swear her face turns as red as the furnace's eyes. Good—that's what I was hoping for.

The second I walk into our bedroom, Jenna hugs me. "Anna! The chair worked great! Roger couldn't get in, but he tried."

We high-five each other.

"I hate that guy."

As I finish putting on another pair of sweatpants, I grab Jenna's hand. "Let's get going to school. I'd rather not hang out in this house any longer than I have to."

The only sound is our footsteps on the pavement as we walk our normal morning route. I'm happy about this because I'm tired and don't know how to fake being happy or want to talk.

The closer I get to school, the sadder I am. Mrs. Swing is not my friend. True friends keep secrets. My wolfpack sisters at Mrs. Dorsey never told anyone anything that I said. Not like Jessica, my foster mother who was super nice, but who also told Mrs. Alex about Curtis and had him moved. I'd thought she was our friend, too, but instead, Mrs. Alex took Curtis. I lost him.

And then there was Daddy. I told him what Derek was doing to me and, the next day, Mrs. Alex came and took me away because Daddy said he couldn't protect me anymore. I should never have told those people anything. I thought Mrs. Swing would be different. She was a foster kid. I thought that made her special—and I could trust her.

Mrs. Swing stands in the class's doorway. Great, I have to walk by her. *Ugh.* I hope she doesn't say anything. I don't want to talk to her right now.

"Ah. Um. Anna? Good morning." Mrs. Swing has a surprised look on her face.

I hope she knows that I know what she did to me.

Just Another Door

I say nothing as I walk past her. I watch her out of the corner of my eye. Though she's talking with other students at the door, she keeps looking in my direction.

"Hi, Anna," says Marie. "It's going to be nice today. Do you want to be my partner at recess today for hopscotch?"

"Sure, Marie, that sounds like fun."

Everyone seems off this morning. Normally, Marie would talk nonstop, just like Jenna. But she wasn't talking a lot, this morning either. Does everyone know that I don't want them to talk to me?

My teacher tries to make eye contact all morning, but I look away. Her smile fades each time I do.

"After lunch, I'd like to see the following students at my desk: James, Debbie, Barb, Tom, Anna, Mark, Forrest, Jessica, Elizabeth, Joseph, and Marie," she says. "I'll call you up one at a time so we can finish up reviewing grades. Enjoy your recess."

Most of the kids go flying through the door to get out and escape school. I'm not that excited but I sure wish I was because Mrs. Swing steps in front of me before I leave the classroom.

"I wasn't expecting to see you this morning, but I'm glad I did." She smiles.

It must be a shock for her since her little tattletale should have gotten me sent to a different foster home and school. If I can't trust a foster kid, then I can absolutely not trust anyone.

"Yup." is all I can say without crying. I walk past her and don't look back. My heart hurts. How could she do that to me? How?

"Anna, come on! We're ready to play!" Marie yells from across the playground.

Great. Marlene's standing at the hopscotch board. I have a feeling this will not be good for me today because I'm too tired to deal with her crap, and when I'm tired, I'm grumpy.

Marlene yells, "No! I don't want to play with Scumbag Girl!"

My blood is heating up, and *I* try to remind myself she's not worth it, but that's not working today. "Shut the hell up, Marlene, before I beat the crap out of you! I don't care if I spend the *week* in the basement, so stay out of my way!" I clench my fists and take a step toward her, staring into her eyes.

She backs off. "You're not worth my time. I don't want to get my hands dirty by touching you." Of course, Marlene has to say something back. She always does.

That's it. I'm going to knock her lights out.

I take a few more steps toward her, this time, with my fists in the air.

Marie steps in between us. "Let's get the game going." Marie hands me the rock to throw. "Don't fight her. Come with me."

I follow Marie to where the rest of our team stands.

"You'll never beat me, Scumbag," she taunts me, then throws her rock. It lands on number four.

I'm glad I didn't get that number because it's hard for me to bed down on one foot and pick it up.

Malene falls over and touches other numbers with her foot. She's out.

My turn. My rock lands on number eight. Yay! Easy Peasy. I can't fall over. I have to beat this girl at this game, and today is the day.

I don't fall. Matter of fact, I make it all the way back with the rock without making a mistake. "Wahoo! I just whipped your butt, Marlene!"

She walks over to me and stops in my face. "You think you're such hot stuff, but all you are is an unwanted foster kid that no one wants. How does it feel to be a reject and a retard at the same time? Momma says that you're stupid in school."

I stand firm. My nails are digging into my clenched fist. This girl wants me to punch her. She wouldn't say such horrible things if she didn't? But I'm not gonna. Instead, I step closer, and put my nose against hers. "I'd rather be a foster kid then have a wicked witch as a mother like you do. I think I'm way luckier than you are."

The kids around me start laughing." Look! Anna's going to kiss Marlene!"

"No, she's not, stupid. Anna's telling her off. Go, Anna!" Marie screams in support.

I stand strong. I'm like a dog right now trying to be alpha. I'm not going to move. I stare into her ugly blue eyes. Then—

Marlene backs away. "This is stupid. Your breath stinks." She looks at her friends. "C'mon, guys. Let's get away from the dirty kids." They follow her like lost puppies.

It feels good to stand up for myself. This way is better than punching her. I won't get a night in the basement for this. But I shrug. I don't care anymore about the punishment because I'll just go to my fort.

I'm not happy when recess ends because I have to be around Mrs. Swing and that makes me feel both sad and mad.

My teacher sticks to her word and calls students up to her desk. I'm the last one.

I sit down in the chair and look at the floor. I don't want to look at her. I don't want to talk to her, and I don't want to be this close to her. I'm heating up; I can feel it.

"Anna, I'd like to talk to you about why you're upset with me."

I say nothing. But she's wrong—I'm not upset; I'm pissed.

"Anna, did your caseworker visit your house last night?"

I nod.

"What happened?"

Though I'm sitting next to her desk and kids are all around me, I feel like…

Like I'm all alone in blackness. Now no one can help me, and no one can understand. Though many people are around, it's just… me.

Chapter 9
The Flashlight

"Anna, unfortunately, I had to call your caseworker yesterday morning because Principal Jim said I had to." Mrs. Swing watches me. "I had to report that your foster parents are mistreating you."

No, she didn't. She told me I could trust her and then... I couldn't.

Mrs. Swing sighs. "Anna, believe me, I never meant to betray your trust or make you unhappy. I'm required by my job to report the ab— mistreatment, and I really want to help you find a nice foster home. You deserve that, Anna Snow."

No kidding. But I don't think there *are* any nice foster homes. Well, Momma Johnson's was nice, but then my stupid birth mother—who didn't even want me—had to make me leave.

I can't trust anyone.

Mrs. Swing scooches a little closer to me. "I would never do anything on purpose to hurt your trust in me. I know that, in foster care, it's hard to trust people. But I really do want what's best for you."

She touches my arm, but I yank it back. I don't like people touching me and I especially don't like people who tell me I can trust them and then tell on me.

"Since you're here today, I'm assuming nothing happened with your foster parents?"

"No, nothing happened. Even though I told my caseworker about the basement, she didn't believe me." I lower my head. I'm *not* going to cry. No one will ever see me cry. How is anyone supposed to help me if they all think I'm a liar? Does Mrs. Alex think that foster parents don't lie?

"Are you *kidding* me?" Mrs. Swing slams her hand on the desk. "Did your caseworker talk with you?"

"Yes. She and the foster parents talked with me."

"Together? Did she talk with all of you *together*?"

"Yup."

"Anna, that's *not* okay. She should've talked with you by yourself."

I shrug because it wouldn't have changed things. "Well, she didn't. Mrs. Alex never believes me. She called me a liar like she always does when I tell her the bad things that happen. She only believes the foster parents."

Mrs. Swing shakes her head. "Anna, that's not right. What can I do to help you?"

What she can do is not tell my secrets. She thought she was helping, but she actually made things worse.

"I'm good. I don't need you to help me."

"Can I ask you where you slept last night after the caseworker visited?"

What am I supposed to tell her? If I tell the truth, will she call Mrs. Alex, and I'll get in trouble again? "Um… I… um… slept in my room."

"Anna, please. I know you think you can't trust me because I had to report their ab—mistreatment, but I promise you, you *can* share anything with me."

No, I can't. "I'm good." She might think she's doing the right thing by telling Mrs. Alex, but if I hafta sleep in the basement again, that'll leave Jenna alone and I can't let Roger do to her what Derek did to me. "I'm okay, Mrs. Swing. Thank you for caring. Can I go back to my desk, please?"

Mrs. Swing looks at me for a few more seconds. I don't move because I'm trying really hard not to cry. I can't cry in front of her or she'll know I'm lying, and I just can't deal with whatever Mrs. Alex or Roger will do.

"Okay then. On to something else." She flips open her grade book. "We need to go over your grades."

Oh boy. Here it comes. As if I don't have enough bad stuff going on right now. But I have to go along with this, so she doesn't ask any more questions about the basement. "Okay."

"You've only had a few grades, but I see you are not completing your homework. Does anyone do work with you at your house?"

Jane asks about it, but she forgets to follow up because she's too busy sending me to the basement for the night, but Mrs. Swing doesn't need that information because she'll probably just tell Mrs. Alex. "Everyone in the house is busy and I just forget about having homework. It's only been a few days at school." How can missing a few assignments impact anything so far?

"I see." She taps her desk. "I have the study hall support all set up for you with Ms. Deborah. I know it's only been two days days with us, but, so far, you've handed in nothing. I don't want you to get too far behind. It makes it harder to stay current."

"Do I have to go? I don't want kids to make fun of me."

My teacher's face turns stern. "This is not an option. I'm not going to allow you to fail fifth grade. We have the entire year together, so I want us and you to get off on the right foot. Getting behind in your homework and your grades is *not* the best way to do that." Mrs. Swing taps the desk with the eraser on her pencil, then closes her book. "Anna, let me make this clear—you having someone to talk to is more important to me than calling Mrs. Alex. I tried that, and it didn't work for you. So, I'm here to help you in any way I can. Please don't close me out. I remember doing that when I was in foster care. I really *do* want to help."

I was hoping she would say that.

"And then, as to the matter of your grades… You are *not* going to fail my class, got it?" She wrinkles her face, making her eyes cross.

I giggle. "Got it." Mrs. Swing likes to make faces to get kids to laugh. It works for me.

"Go back to your seat. I'll call you up at the end of the day to take the attendance record to the office. But, before you go, I'd like to give you this."

She hands me a little flashlight thing.

Just Another Door

I've never seen one this small before. I hold it up. "This is neat."

She chuckles. "It is. I carry that flashlight in my car in case I need it. But I think this is something that would be perfect for you to have if you have to spend a night in the basement. Can you find a place to hide it down there?"

"Yes. The basement floor is dirt, so I can bury it."

"Great idea." She gives me a thumbs-up.

I slide it into my pants pocket. This is perfect. Maybe Mrs. Swing isn't so bad after all. I'm feeling so much better. I didn't lose my teacher as my friend, and she's still trying to help me.

"Okay, class. Time for math. Our last subject of the day. Books out." Mrs. Swing is all teacher-like again up at the front of the classroom.

How lucky I am to have her as my teacher. I'm still not sure what's happening to me, a confusing mess of different emotions, but at least I'm happy in her class.

"Anna, can you come to my desk and get the attendance report and carry that to the office, please?"

I stand slowly. I'll do whatever I can to not draw attention to myself. I hate that.

"'Bye, Anna," says Marie. "I'll see you tomorrow. We can play hopscotch."

"Sounds good, Marie." I wave 'bye.

I follow Mrs. Swing to her desk. She hands me a file folder and whispers, "Good luck today."

I head to the office.

Ms. Diane, the secretary, is all smiles when I show up. "Hi, Anna. I can take that report. Ms. Deborah will be with you in a second."

The wooden chair is hard on my bum. Shouldn't schools have comfortable seats if kids have to sit in them all day? That could be why we have a hard time staying seated in class. The room is filled with boxes of papers, and pictures of kids in sports all over the place. I stand to look at the picture of the baseball teams, remembering when I played baseball. It'd made my brother mad that I was better at it than he was.

"Hello, Anna. "Let's go over this way."

A voice brings me out of my thoughts and

I follow Ms. Deborah into a small room that has posters on the wall. One says, *You are free to make your own choices.*

Yeah… that's not true for foster kids. We don't get to decide which

93

foster parents we want to live with. Caseworkers should give us a choice—tell us about three or four families and let us pick. And we ought to be able to leave any foster home for any reason.

"Do you like that poster, Anna?"

"Yup."

Ms. Deborah walks over to it. "Can you read this out loud for me?"

"Nope."

Ms. Deborah's eyebrows raise. "Okay, then can you share with me why you don't *want* to read it for me?"

I cock my head. I hate reading out loud and feel dumb when I do it. Plus, kids always laugh at me when I mess up words. Back in first grade, my teacher tested my intelligence—*in front of the class*. I was mad because I didn't want to do it, so I gave her the wrong answers on purpose. Reading is hard for me.

Then, that teacher had had me put puzzles together. Even though I knew how to, I still played dumb because I hadn't wanted to do it. I'd wanted to do the art project with all the other kids, not stupid testing.

Ugh, my teachers are always giving me so much to do! I think, sometimes, that they're just waiting for me to mess up. I always get Fs; they say my work is terrible. It seems I'm not good at anything when it comes to school, so why bother trying to do schoolwork when I'm only going to move, anyway? I don't need school to show me why people are mean to me. I'm nobody and I don't belong with any family or any school.

"Anna?"

Ugh. I have to come up with an answer. "I, uh, just don't like reading out loud."

"I see." Ms. Deborah pulls out a chair for me to sit down. "I didn't like to read out loud when I was your age, either. Kids would laugh at me."

"Really?".

"Yupper. That's why I became a teacher, so I can help kids who struggle like I did.

"That's cool." I like Ms. Deborah. She and Mrs. Swing remind me of me. They became a teacher so they can help kids because of what happened to them. When I get older, maybe I'll like reading and find a way to help foster kids.

"Anna, this quote is one of my favorites. *You are free to make your own choices.* It means that working hard in school can open doors to any future you can imagine." She sits across from me. "What would you like to be when you grow up?"

"Um... I want to do something for animals." Animals like me and they don't hurt me.

"Perhaps you'll be a veterinarian."

"What's that?"

"A doctor who works with animals. They help heal them."

Hmm. Ms. Deborah's on to something because I'd love to help injured animals. "Do you gotta be smart to do that?"

"You need to do well in school to learn how to help them."

"Oh. Okay. Then, yes, I'd like to be a vet... rin... scarian."

Ms. Deborah giggles. "It's a tough word to pronounce, and I struggle with it, too."

We both crack up, trying to say it quickly.

"Okay, no rush on the reading; we have plenty of time. But let's take a look at your math homework. When we're done with it, I'll give it to Mrs. Swing so you won't have to worry about lugging it home and then bringing it back tomorrow. Does that plan sound good?"

"Okay." Having help with math is not a bad thing. It's a worse subject for me than reading. If someone is going to help me, I should let them, right? Or does that depend? I don't have to let someone like Roger help me because he's just trying to do something else. Ms. Deborah is helping just because she wants to.

The time with Ms. Deborah goes fast, and it's nice having help with my worst subject ever. I never knew that I'd like fractions.

"Great job, Anna. I'll give this to Mrs. Swing. Have a good night and I'll see you on Monday. Have an enjoyable weekend."

She waves and I'm out the door. Another school day done—Holy moly! My first week at my new school *flew* by. This foster home feels like it's lasted forever. Only a week? I can't believe it! Thinking about my prison-like foster home is awful, so I try to distract myself by thinking about other things. Like... I can't wait to see the kitten again.

I'd planned to sneak my lunch milk to the kitten when Jenna and I get home, but Roger's waiting for us.

"Ah, my favorite special girl is home!" he says, staring at her in a way I never want anyone to look at me—or my friend—ever again.

Yeah, he's not waiting for me.

"I brought you something…" He hands Jenna a big candy bar.

"Where's mine?" I smirk because I know what game he's playing. The same one my foster mother, Sue, played on me. But I'm never falling for the "special gifts" game again. That only ends up badly—for me. I don't want the same thing to happen to Jenna.

"Sorry, Anna, I only had money for one." His greasy hair hangs on his pimply forehead. He always looks sweaty.

"Don't worry, Anna, I'll share it with you."

I wanna yell at Jenna not to take it. I don't blame her, though; it looks good. But that's what Roger wants us to think about.

"Uh, where's Jane?" I ask him as he stares at Jenna and me like we're ice cream cones.

"She and Barry took Marlene to the doctor." He points to the back porch. "I'd like you to clean the back porch, Anna. Jenna, you can come with me, and I'll teach you how to clean a toilet." He points to the upstairs bathroom. "Jane wanted me to show you how to do that."

The kitten will have to wait. There's no way I'm leaving Jenna with him.

Jenna steps on my foot as she practically melts into me.

Yeah, I'm not letting him get away with this. "Sorry, Roger, but I need Jenna's help for my science class. She's going to help me find leaves and then draw them on paper. We will be busy all night 'til Jane gets home. And you know how mad she'll get if we don't do our homework." I grab Jenna's hand. "Thank you for helping me. Let's go."

I lead her through the kitchen and out the back door. "Don't say anything 'til we're outside," I whisper.

"Thanks for getting me away from him, Anna. But I thought you said you didn't need my help."

"I wasn't going to leave you with him. No way! Come on, I want to show you something. But, before I do, you have to pinky-swear that you won't tell anyone about it." I put my pinky up. She won't tell anyone about the kitten after giving me her bear for the basement. We're in this together.

She locks her finger with mine. "I swear."

"Good. Follow me." I walk her to the metal doors on the outside of the house. "These things go to the basement." I point to the handle. "And see that? No lock. I can lift them."

Jenna's mouth drops open. "Whoa. I never saw those before."

"That's because they're on the back of the house. Has any other foster kid ever told you they could get out of the basement?"

Jenna looks up at the sky. "Nope. Never."

"Well, I did get out. Those doors go into that really dark room down there that Jane said to stay out of."

Jenna nods. "Yeah, she said there's a well in that room, and we could fall in and get hurt."

Hmmm... Jane didn't say that to me. I didn't see one, but maybe it's there and Jane was hoping I'd fall into it.

"Well, then, it's a good thing I have this." I pull out the flashlight. "My teacher gave this to me in case Jane locks me in the basement again." I raise my eyebrows. "You and I both know that *will* happen."

She giggles with me. "Yup, Anna, I bet it will."

"The next time I'm in the basement, I'll bury this under the dirt by the blue door. I'll find something to sit on top of it so you can find where to dig to get it if you ever get sent down there."

She claps her hands. "Great idea! That makes me feel so much better."

I agree. *Thank you, Mrs. Swing.*

"C'mon, let's get away from these doors so Roger doesn't see us standing here. We don't want him to realize our escape plan." We go behind a car in the driveway. "When you come out of the doors, run as fast as you can to this spot." I show her where to kneel down, then point to the woods. "See how close we are now? But you have to make sure no one is outside before you run." This time, I'm the one grabbing Jenna's hand as we run into the woods.

"Here, kitty kitty! Here, kitty kitty!" I pat my leg, hoping the kitten hears me.

"Is there a cat around here?" Jenna gets excited, like me.

"Yep. I saw it last night when I was in the woods."

"Wait." Jenna stops walking. "You were in the *woods* last night?"

Did she not hear me explain about the doors? "Yup. I snuck out of the basement through those doors." I smack the giant tree we're standing in front of. "I climbed this big boy and sat on that branch." We both look up to where I point. I didn't realize how high it was.

"Whoa, Anna! Weren't you afraid you'd fall down? It's so high up."

"I know. But it was so cool. I could see everyone walking around in the dining room. When I climbed down, I found a pretty white kitten." I walk around a little, calling it over and over, but it doesn't come. I hope nothing happened to it. "Jenna, let me show you something else, but we have to walk through the woods and down a hill. Are you okay with that?"

"Let's do it."

I lead her to the tree house.

"Hey, let's go check it out!"

Of *course,* the moment we start our hike, we hear the sound of Jane's car.

We stop dead in our tracks.

"Well, darn it. Jane might really want us to clean. We better head home. But, remember, you and I were doing science class. We have to have the same story." I scoop up some leaves to make it believable.

"Got it." She grabs some, too.

"Okay. Let's walk down the side of the woods and then out onto the driveway in case she's trying to find us."

"Okay. Good thinking." Jenna checks to see if Jane's looking for us.

"Where the heck are the kids?" I can hear Jane yelling as we walk up the driveway.

She comes out of the house and heads toward her car, but stops when she catches sight of Jenna and me. "Where the heck were you kids?"

"We went for a walk to look for leaves for my science class." I show her my collection, and so does Jenna. "Jenna's helping me."

"Well, get inside. I need to talk to you both. I had a word with your teachers today."

Uh oh. Did Mrs. Swing tell Jane anything else? I hope not; she said I could trust her.

We head to the house, leave the leaves on the porch like she tells us to, then head to the dining room—

Where Roger is. Ugh.

"Hi, Jenna. Have a seat by me while we're waiting for Mom," he pats the chair next to him.

"That's okay, Roger," I say. I'm not giving him any chance to touch her. "I want Jenna to sit next to me."

She follows me to the other side of the table where we sit side-by-side—almost on top of each other, really.

Roger drums his fingers on the table and gives us a creepy smile. "There's no need for you two sweethearts to sit that far away. I won't bite. I like to kiss instead. That's what daddies do with their daughters."

He makes me want to vomit. "Well, I guess we don't have to worry about that then, because you're not our daddy."

"Be careful what you say, little lady, if you don't want another visit to the basement."

He has no idea that the basement is actually a treat for me now that I can get out of it and go into the woods.

Jane walks in and looks at him, then at us. "Am I missing something?"

She's so clueless. She's missing *every*thing—including that her husband likes little girls.

"Nope, honey, just telling the girls that we need to talk." He grabs Jane's hand.

"We sure do." She sits down.

"Mom! Do you have a cold washcloth?" Marlene yells down from somewhere in the house. Probably her stupid pink bedroom.

"In the bathroom, honey. I'll be up soon." Jane turns off that stupid smile she had when talking to her daughter to glare at me.

Not that she looks at me in any other way anymore.

I feel the same.

"So." She links her hands on the table. "Let's start with Anna."

Great. Here it comes.

"Your teacher says that you are doing fantastic and are one of her best students. I had to ask several times to make sure she had the right kid. If this is true, why can't you behave at home?"

She doesn't *really* want me to answer that because, first off, I'd tell her this place ain't my home and never will be. And, second, that she sucks, and that's why I don't want to be nice to her.

But I don't say anything. The basement might not be punishment anymore, but I don't want to leave Jenna alone at night. Not with Roger giving her those creepy looks, even with Jane sitting right here.

"You gonna say anything?" Jane squeezes her fingers together.

"Nope."

Jane shakes her head. "Fine. But the next time you're hurt, you can show *us* rather than complaining to the school nurse."

Huh, I *did* tell her, and she did nothing about it. Is she just acting dumb right now?

"Now, Jenna, let's talk about my conversation with your teacher. Let's just say that you will have the night in the basement tonight to think about what you can do differently in school."

Jenna squeezes my leg, and I know why—what if Roger sneaks into the basement while she's down there by herself?

Looks like I'll be in the basement *with* her tonight.

"What did I do, Momma Jane?" Jenna whines.

I want to yell at her to stop, but I say nothing. I don't want her to let Jane see that she's scared of her or upset by her threats. I want Jenna to be strong. She *has* to be strong to survive foster care. If you're weak, you'll die in this system.

"Your teacher says that you're falling asleep in class most days and that you're not turning in your homework."

I want to scream that Jenna might sleep at night if she wasn't so afraid of Jane's terrible husband, but what's the point? Jenna hasn't said anything, so there's no reason for Jane to believe me. No one ever does anyway.

"Take your school things upstairs, then head to the basement, young lady."

Jenna goes upstairs, crying, while I stay at the table.

"What is it with you foster kids? We give you a home and you don't appreciate it," she says.

I sooooo want to tell her it's because her home sucks, but I won't. Because it won't change anything.

After I push in my chair, I head to our bedroom. Jenna is already putting warmer pants on. "I'll keep this light so I can crawl into the basement with you. I won't let you stay in there alone all night. It's Friday anyway and we don't have school tomorrow."

Jenna tucks the bear into her pants. "You'll do that for me?"

"Of course. We can think of it as our own little adventure. Plus, I'll take the milk to see if we can find the kitten."

"Our own little adventure." Jenna smiles now.

"Yeah, but, Jenna, don't walk into the dark room without me. I didn't see a well, but it could be there. We're gonna need my flashlight because the bear's isn't strong enough to scope out the entire room, okay?"

"Yeah, that's a good idea. Thank you so much, Anna, for doing this for me! I don't want to be down there in case…"

Neither of us says it, but we're both thinking about it.

Yeah, I'm not leaving her down there alone.

She gives me a big hug. Gosh, she reminds me so much of Curtis. Like I did for him, I'll protect her.

Just Another Door

"Get down here, Jenna!" Jane screeches—like always.
Jenna runs to the door fast. "I gotta go, Anna."
"Go on. And I'll get you some food on the sly and bring it along."
"Thanks, Anna. See you later."
Yes, she will.
Because she's not alone anymore. She has a sister.

Chapter 10
Tree House Fort

I'm so ready for this awful long dinner to be over; every moment feels like an eternity. As soon as I can, I need to get Jenna some food. I bet she's hungry now.

"Pass the buns, please, Anna."

We've got little Barry with us this weekend.

"Get ready to catch, Barry." I giggle, tossing the bread across the table.

"Anna, knock it off." Of course Jane yells at me. "I don't know what the heck you did in your other foster homes, but in this one, we don't throw food."

Ignoring her, I wink at Barry.

Everyone's finally done eating. Normally, I would have left already and gone to my room, but, today, I had to eat slowly and wait for everyone to finish because I need to grab food for Jenna. "Jane, I can clean up the table if you like."

Everyone looks at me because, yeah, I haven't done this before.

"Are you trying to be the good kid now? You are *so* weird." Marlene drops her fork onto her plate, sending some of the noodles flying.

Any other time, I'd be pissed at her making a mess for me to clean up, but I can't let her make me angry so I end up in my room all night. I mean, I might go off on her if I *knew* Jane would send me to the basement *with* Jenna, but she's not that nice. Or clueless. No, I need to stay calm so I can follow through with my plan.

Jane hands me her plate. "Good. About time you earned your keep. Do you know where the containers are located?

"Yes, I do." No, I don't, but I need some time alone in the kitchen. I'll figure it out; I always do.

"Okay then." She grabs Roger's hand, "Leave your dishes on the table and Anna can clean it all up. Let's go for a walk."

Perfect! Once I get rid of them, I'll unlock the blue door and pass the food to Jenna. 'Course, I'm gonna have to watch out for Marlene.

I find the plastic food containers, then scoop up a huge pile of spaghetti and toss it in with a spoon, then I go look for Marlene.

Luckily, she's on her bed, listening to music and writing something. That ought to give me some time.

I dash downstairs and look out the window to see if I can see Jane or Roger in the driveway.

Nope. Good. That means they're far from the house.

I rush downstairs, unlock the blue door, and find Jenna sobbing. "Hey, Jenna. Don't cry. I'm not gonna let you be alone tonight, but I have to go before Jane catches me. Here's some dinner. I'll see you later." I put the food on the dirt floor, then lock the door and run back up the wooden stairs.

"Anna?"

I freeze. Why is Barry looking for me? And why does it have to be *now*? I can't just walk out or answer him because he'll know I'm on the stairs and he will *definitely* mention it to Jane or Marlene, even if it's by accident.

I hang out on the top step, waiting for him to go somewhere else in the house.

"Marlene!" He heads toward the living room.

I get out of the stairwell without making a sound. Phew. I did it! Now, to make myself busy cleaning up because—Yup. Just what I thought. Marlene runs in, all out of breath.

"Where the hell were you?" She slams her hands onto her hips like she's in charge.

"Where the hell do you think I was?" *Sorry, Jesus. I know you don't like me to swear, but, sometimes, I just hafta.*

"Barry said he came into the kitchen and didn't see you."

I don't want to call little Barry a liar, so I gotta figure out a way to get out of this one. "Maybe he came in when I was in the bathroom, washing my hands. He wouldn't see me, *Weirdo*, if the door's shut." Now *I'm* the one putting my hands on my hips, giving *her* attitude.

Marlene rolls her eyes. "How nice; Animal can pee in the human potty. She's housebroken." She laughs at herself.

"Marlene, do you want me as your girlfriend or something? Is that way you spend so much effort on me?" I have the biggest grin on my face because I know just how she's gonna react—which is why I said this. Marlene thinks she's smarter than me? Ha. She has no idea what I'm capable of.

"Eww! You're gross!" She whips her hair as she disappears out of the kitchen.

My heart pounds so hard and fast, I need to sit down as the room spins. It reminds me of when I used to pass out. I haven't done that in a long time. And I can't now. I need to help my sister.

But the room spins faster and fast…

I'm swimming in a pool, diving deep in the water and touching the bottom. How I love to swim. I wish the foster home would have a pool.

"Anna!'

Ouch. What? I rub my cheek where it hurts. What happened?

"Wake up, Anna. Wake up, damn it!"

I open my eyes. "Jane?" Her face is close to mine. "Did you… *hit* me?"

"I had to because your ass is on the ground. What the hell happened?"

"I must've passed out. I used to do that a lot," I whisper.

"Well, get up." Jane tugs my arms to get me moving.

Before long, I'm sitting on my bum.

"I'll call the doctor. We need to get these things checked out. I don't need something happening to you and have the state blaming us for it."

I have no clue what she's talking about, but, right now, I couldn't care less because the room keeps spinning.

Just Another Door

"And I guess *I'll* have to finish these myself while I wait for the doctor to call back." Jane almost smashes a dish to smithereens.

I'll probably get blamed for that if it breaks. "Um… I can do that, Jane." Not really, since both Jane and the room are a blur. I told her I would do it and I don't want her to yell at me later for not doing something I said I'd do.

"Anna, it's bedtime. Go get some sleep after that episode."

Shaky legs and all, I head to our room, then lie down on Jenna's bed because I probably shouldn't climb up to mine. I really wanna stay here and not move, but that'll make me fall asleep and I can't do that. I told Jenna I wouldn't let her be alone.

My foster parents' bedroom door finally shuts so I can make good on my promise.

I open our bedroom window, then feel around for the ladder I'd put against the house.

Got it! One step at a time, I climb down. Then, keeping low so no one can see me out of a window, I run toward the basement doors.

I make it without getting caught! I open one of the doors. It creaks a little, but not loud enough to wake anyone.

I slide inside, then pull out the flashlight. Time to find Jenna.

"Hey, Jenna, I'm here," I whisper as loudly as I can without being loud enough for anyone upstairs to hear. I can't get caught now.

I turn the corner and—ohmygod. I want to punch Jane in the face because Jenna's all curled up and is as white as a ghost.

"Jenna…" I walk over, trying not to scare her.

She leaps up when she sees me. "Anna! You came!"

"'Course I did; I told you I would."

Jenna's probably like me and doesn't trust what people say. In foster care, people say all kinds of things and make all sorts of promises, then never follow through. Foster care is a promise-breaker for a lot of us.

"Do you want to get out of here for a little while?"

"Sure do!" Jenna grabs my hand.

"First, let's see if there's a well in the black room, so's we know if we have to be really careful. Stay behind me." I shine the light everywhere as we creep in.

In the far back corner, I see what looks like a huge opening in the dirt. "That way, Jenna. I think that might be the well."

We walk over carefully, and, yup, it's a huge black hole in the ground. "Stay here, Jenna. I'll be right back."

I inch closer and shine my light into it. There's water a ways down in this hole. Jane was actually telling the truth. "This thing is huge. We hafta be careful 'cause if we fall in, there's no way to get out."

"Be careful, Anna. I don't want you to fall in," Jenna says.

Yeah, this is crazy scary. "We better check to see if there's anything else we need to worry about."

I shine the light around and—"Whoa! There's another hole over there! No way!"

"What if something crawls out of that hole, Anna?"

I was just thinking the same thing, but I can't let her know I'm scared. I promised I'd protect her, so I have to at least pretend to be brave.

I walk to the other hole and shine the flashlight in. "Well, I don't think anything's gonna crawl out 'cause the bottom is too far down." Sheesh, if I had gone the wrong way with the bear last night, I could have fallen into one of these wells and wouldn't have been able to get out. I don't even know how deep the water is, so... I could have drowned, maybe.

Just thinking about it gives me chills. I've never been so creeped out.

I head back to Jenna, shining the flashlight all over the floor. "Jenna, if you ever try to get out of here on your own, keep your hand on the wall and follow it to the stairs, since those wells are on the other side of the room." I grab her hand. "Let's get out of here. Here, hold the flashlight so I can open the door."

She shines the light so I can see what I'm doing and I'm able to lift one—

Bam! It slips from my hands and slams down. Oh crap!

We both freeze, listening for footsteps upstairs.

Nothing.

"I don't hear anyone, Anna. I think we're good."

I open the door carefully this time. We both look up at the sky.

Ahh. The smell of fall and leaves; I love it.

"Anna, this is so cool. There are so many stars in the sky."

She's right; it's beautiful and bright enough with the moon. We don't need to use the flashlight now.

"Let's go this way. I wanna show you the fort." Carefully, we walk through the forest. We need to use the flashlight now because the trees block the light from the moon and stars. The beam cuts through the darkness, showing the knotty tree roots and uneven ground. I can't decide what's worse: the blackness that surrounds me, or the eerie creaks and snaps echoing everywhere.

"Did you hear that noise?" Jenna stops walking and takes a deep breath.

I heard it, too; a loud *crack* echoing through the trees as something enormous steps on a branch. "It's nothing. Maybe something fell off one of these trees. We just have to get to the top of that little hill."

After she takes a few steps, Jenna's standing next to me and squeezing my hand. "I don't want to walk behind you anymore. Hold on."

As we stop for a second on the knoll, the chilling sound of howling fills the air, sending goosebumps all over my body. I love dogs, but these sound more like the wolves in scary movies.

"What the heck is that, Anna?"

I can't tell Jenna that I think it's wolves 'cause she'll be scared. "Sounds like dogs. Maybe there are some wild dogs that like to walk around in the woods. Dogs love me, so I don't think they'd hurt us." I stop talking for a second to listen. Maybe their sound can tell me how close they are.

Again, they howl.

They're close. "Let's get moving, Jenna. We don't want to stand here and wait for them to come to us."

"Okay, let's go."

My hand starts to throb from Jenna's grip, but I can't say if I blame her. We went from one scary place to another. I knew the woods would be freaky at night, but I had no idea it would be this bad.

Finally, we reach the fort. "You climb up first, Jenna, and then I'll follow. It'll be dark up there, but I've been here before and it's okay."

"Okay." Jenna starts her climb. But she's slow as the ladder moves around on her.

I'm close to screaming at her to hurry because I can hear those wolves getting closer; they're practically behind me!

A sharp rock catches my attention. We'll need this in the fort. I scoop it up quickly. I need to keep an eye on what's behind me in case the wolves show up. I can't stand here for those things to eat me.

Thankfully, we finally get into the fort, but those howling dogs keep reminding us we aren't alone tonight.

"Anna, how close are they, do you think?"

"I don't know. It feels like they are right under us." I walk out onto the little porch area to shine the light down. I don't see anything, but—wow! That is a long way down. I can't believe I even *thought* about jumping last night to join Jesus. If I fell, I'd get seriously hurt and be dinner for those wolves. That wouldn't be a nice way to go.

I take a few steps back because I have no idea how old this place is and it might rot out from under me.

"There's nothing out here," I say as I head back to her. "But look at this place—isn't it great?" I show her all the initials. "Guess what I brought with me?" I pull out the sharp rock. "Now we get to join the club!"

I scratch into the wood: *Jenna & Anna were here*. I will always be alive in this fort with my name carved into it. The place where I thought about jumping so I could die. The place where I changed my mind and decided to live so I can make things better for foster kids. The place that has my name on it.

"Let's chill here a sec and see if the dogs will wander off if we're quiet." I'm still freaking out because it sounds like there's an enormous pack of them. And they could, for sure, take Jenna and me.

"Good idea, Anna."

I flop onto the wood floor, my legs all twisted up like pretzels. I'm so tired, I don't even know how long I sit here before I fall asleep.

"Anna, I'm freezing." I eyes jolt open at her voice. . Her skin is as cold as ice.

"Should we head back to the basement?" I'd rather not, but if Jenna says yes, I guess we will.

"No way, Anna! Those dogs are still howling. Do you think they're wolves?"

"Yes, that's exactly what they are. How about we stay here 'til the sun comes up? We can sneak back into the basement before Jane wakes up."

"Yes, let's do that. Jane sleeps in late on weekends, so we'll have plenty of time to get back."

I have to trust Jenna since I haven't been here long enough to know otherwise.

My new sister wraps her arms around me, and I do the same to her. Though we both have sweatpants and sweatshirts on, it's still cold out here. Even if we don't wake up, we are not prisoners to Jane. We are deciding where we want to be to sleep. It feels better than having to stay in the basement because *we* get to choose it for us.

I jump up when Jenna screams, "Oh no! We slept too long! We gotta go!"

The birds are singing away like they don't have a care in the world, and I wish I can say that, but Jane's gonna lose her mind when she finds out that we found a way out of the basement.

We climb down the ladder, then run toward the top of the hill—just in time to see Roger driving away with Marlene.

I stop Jenna. "Wait. Let Roger get out of the driveway first."

We duck behind some bushes and wait for him to pass, then we sprint toward the house.

Darn, the kitchen lights are on, but, thankfully, no one's in the window. We run our route by the car; then head for the basement.

"Anna, aren't you going to close the door?" Jenna asks as I follow her back down the stairs.

"Nope, no time. I gotta get your dish." If Jane gets to the basement before we do, she'll see the dish I brought down. That'll be a sure giveaway that I disobeyed her.

The flashlight guides us through the black room, back to Jenna's spot. Footsteps are loud above our heads. I grab the dish and, as I run into the dark room, I throw it into one of the well holes. It lands with a loud *Splash!*. I hope Jane doesn't hear it.

I run as fast as I can to get up the steps before Jane opens the blue door for Jenna.

The door to the outside creaks when I shut it. I run to duck behind the car, trying to catch my breath just as Jane screams my name. Phew! Just made it!

"Anna, where the hell are you?"

I'm not gonna answer. I wait 'til she goes back into the house, then I run to the driveway, walking up it like nothing's wrong.

I do grab more leaves so I can say I was out picking them up for my class.

I open the front door slowly 'cause if Jane doesn't hear me, I can sneak up to my room and pretend to have been somewhere else in the house. I know how to act dumb.

"Anna? Is that you?"

So much for that plan. "Yep, it's me."

Jane comes into the foyer, her face all red. "What the hell, Anna? It's after ten. How early did you get up this morning?"

Stay calm. I look down at the leaves in my hands. "I dunno. I just like being outside." That *is* the truth, so I don't have to lie about that.

"I spent all morning looking for you, even outside. Didn't you hear me calling you?"

"Nope." That, too, is the truth. "Is Jenna upstairs now?"

Jane waves her hand in the air. "Head upstairs and do whatever you want to do today."

I *wish* I could do whatever I want. I certainly wouldn't spend it in my room. Or even this house. The *only* good thing about this place is Jenna.

I head up to my bedroom, leaving Jane in my dust.

I put a finger to my mouth when I see Jenna in our room 'cause Jane might be standing at the bottom of the stairs and I don't want her to hear us. I close our door.

Jenna jumps up and down. "No way we got away with that!" Her face lights up with a big smile.

It makes me happy to see her like that. She's like my sister. We high-five each other but then decide to take a nap since we didn't get much sleep. Jane *did* say we could do what we want, so…

I get woken up by a, "Hey there, sweetie."

Who in the world is that?

I slowly roll over and slit my eyes just the tiniest bit.

It's Roger.

I lay perfectly still, my heart pounding. I don't want him to know I'm awake.

That creep is leaning over Jenna's bed *with his private parts hanging out near Jenna's face*!

"It's okay, honey," he says in a creepy, gross voice." You're my special girl. Only special girls can touch me like this."

I listen really hard to hear Jenna. I need all this information because I'm going to do something about it. Maybe I'll stab him with my fork.

"I don't wanna keep doing it."

"I said *keep touching it* and that's what I mean. Otherwise, you'll be in the basement tonight. I'll find *some* way to get you down there." Roger clears his throat, then moans.

I remember Derek and Scott making that sound.

I want to bash him upside the head. Instead, I do the next best thing. "Jane! I don't feel good! Can you come here and help me?!"

I lean my head over the bed, making sure he sees me seeing him.

And I see him all right—he's putting his privates away and zipping up his pants. He looks up at me.

"Get out of our room, Roger, and leave her alone. If you don't, I'll tell Jane about you."

His face turns red. "If you even think about it, young lady, you'll regret it. Maybe I'll teach *you* something all little girls should learn about—how to make a man happy." He winks at me—and not in a joking way—then leaves the room.

Jane comes flying in, just missing her disgusting husband. "What do you need, Anna?".

"Oh, nothing. I wasn't feeling good, but now I am."

"Well, good. I'm glad to hear that because we're having macaroni-and-cheese for dinner." She smiles at me as she leaves the room—I mean, *really* smiles. Like she *likes* me.

Well, that can't be right. What's she up to? Is it because Mrs. Alex came to the house again and she's afraid of getting in trouble? I know she's worried about Marlene having to go live in foster care, so maybe she's trying to be nice so I won't tell anymore things about her.

Well, if she doesn't give me anything to say, I won't have to.

Roger, though…

I jump down to Jenna's bed. She's curled up in a ball and tears are sliding down her cheek. "Does he do that to you a lot?"

She shakes her head. "No. This was the first time. And I don't want to be his special girl or go into that basement with him."

I wrap my arms around her and lie next to her. "Don't worry about the basement, Jenna. I won't leave you alone down there. Ever." I wish I had someone who would look out for me like I do her and did for Curtis. I shrug at the thought. I don't want to be sad anymore when I think about my life. Instead… I'll just have to not need anyone. I'll protect myself if I have to.

I have no idea how long we cuddle before Jane yells about dinner.

"Let's go. I've gotcha, Jenna. I've got you." Together we climb out of bed, the room, and head downstairs.

When we get to the table, everyone is already sitting down and the only two available seats are on either side of Roger.

The creep did this on purpose, so I can't sit next to Jenna

Jenna just spins around to leave the dining room.

"Where are you going, young lady?" Jane asks. She sounds kind.

"I'm not hungry. Can I go back to my room?"

I have no clue how she expects Jane to hear her; I'm right next to her, and *I* can barely hear her.

"Honey, sit down and get some food in that belly."

Jenna heads toward Roger, looking like all her blood has left her body.

I'm not gonna let him get away with this. "Roger, can you move over so I can sit next to Jenna?"

Roger grins at me. "Nope. Take a seat."

The jerk. My favorite food doesn't sound so good anymore.

Jenna sits next to Roger while I sit on the other side.

He chuckles, the creep. He's enjoying this.

"What's so funny, Roger?" Jane asks.

"Nothing, honey. I was remembering something funny that I heard today. No big deal. Nothing to talk about."

While the mac-and-cheese might have been good, I don't like it now—and Jenna doesn't eat it either.

Something hits the bottom of the table hard enough to make the plates jump.

"What the heck was that?" Jane acts shocked by the noise.

I know exactly what that was. Roger's hand must be on Jenna's leg. I gotta help her. "Jenna, do you want to go play outside? I'm done eating, are you?"

Jenna stands up fast. "Yep."

"Excuse me, girls," Jane says. "Just where do you think you're going?"

"I need to get outside because I feel like I might throw up, and I don't want to do it all over the table." I make gagging sounds.

"Me, too." Jenna starts gagging even louder than me.

Jane sighs. "I bet you caught something from school. Well, then, get outside. We do *not* want you throwing up all over our food, and I really don't want to get whatever it is you have." She waves us out and we're more than happy to get out of that room and away from that gross man.

"Are you okay?" I wrap my arm around her shoulder when we're in the driveway.

"Yeah. Roger was playing with my leg again and touching my girl parts." She trembles against me.

"I'm sorry. He's horrible. We have to try to keep you away from him."

Jenna nods.

"Let's head to the fort."

She agrees.

We do our normal routine of hiding behind the car and then making a mad dash for the tree line.

"Anna?"

"Yeah."

"This is my favorite place." She smiles for the first time since our bedroom earlier.

"Me, too, Jenna." We high-five. "And if you ever need to hide, remember that no one knows about this place besides us. I always make sure I have a hiding place in every foster home I live in."

She grabs my arm. "Well, I hope you don't go to any more foster homes. You're like my sister, Anna. You can't leave me."

"Jenna, if I have a choice, I'll never leave you. But if there's some reason I'm not here, run to this hiding spot to get away from Roger."

She says nothing but, instead, nods. Her eyes look sad.

One thing I've learned about foster care is that you never know when you will be moved. I can never promise her that I won't leave because I don't have that choice. Mrs. Alex can show up and move me tomorrow.

"Let's go. It's getting dark, and we don't want to deal with the wolves like we did last night."

"Yup. I don't want to deal with the wolves either." She grabs my hand. I swear her body still shakes from earlier.

"Good night, Jenna," I say to her after climbing into my top bunk. "I'm going to talk with Jesus now before I go to sleep."

"Who's Jesus?" she asks.

"Jesus is in Heaven with God. It's his son. God created the earth and everything on it, including us."

"Wow. That's cool, Anna."

"I know, right? His son, Jesus, was half-god, and his mother was human, like us. He died so we don't have to kill animals anymore when we pray. We can pray right to Jesus. And even though he can't talk to us, he can hear our prayers. He's there to help us. If you believe in him, he will be there for you. I pray to him every night.

"Can you teach me the prayer, Anna?"

"Sure."

Now I lay me down to sleep. I pray to the Lord my soul to keep.
If I should die before I wake, I pray the Lord my soul to take.

Jenna clears her throat. "Thank you, Anna," she says. "That makes me feel better. I'll talk with Jesus like you do."

"Good. Talk to you tomorrow, Jenna." I'm happy I told her about Jesus because maybe it'll help her like it helped me. I feel happy and warm inside. Now I know how Ms. Lisa and Pastor Scott feel after they tell people about Jesus. It feels good.

Chapter 11
Christmas Cookies

"'Morning, girls. Time to get up for school—well, except for you, Anna. You'll be staying with me this morning."

Oh, crud. That doesn't sound good because whenever I hafta stay home from school in a foster home, it usually means that I'm leaving. Please don't let that be the case.

Staying home from school is never a good thing for me. I'm sure today will be no different. I don't like to be around Roger, Jane, or Marlene. And most times when I'm home from school, it's because I'm being moved.

"Anna, get up and get dressed. You'll hang out with me until we have to leave for your doctor's appointment."

"Doctor appointment? Why do I have to do that?" The only time I remember being at a doctor's office is when I got stitches in my hand at my first foster home—and it was *not* fun.

"Let's get you something to eat before we leave." Jane disappears out the door.

Dr. Sharon Zaffarese-Dippold

"I don't like doctors," I mumble, though, honestly, I guess going to the doctor's office is better than being moved out of the home again.

"Me neither. I hate the shots." Jenna shoves her legs into her pants.

"*Shots*? Jenna, do you think I'm getting shots?" I sure hope not.

"Nah. Maybe Mom just wants you to get checked out. She took me, too, when I first got here."

"Did you hafta get shots?"

"Nope, but don't worry, Anna, it'll be okay."

I sure hope so.

Jane doesn't talk to me on the ride; she just sings along to the radio like Mrs. Alex.

Daddy and I used to sing together. He would play Miss Dolly Parton's songs, and we would sing and sing and sing. He even used to call me Dolly.

I miss Daddy.

I miss Curtis.

I miss my church friends and Mama Cat and Thunder.

Why do I hafta keep leaving everything and everyone I love?

"We're here." Jane parks the car.

I look out. I was so busy thinking about Daddy and Curtis and all, I didn't think about where we were going.

But now I do. Shots. I do *not* want them.

The doctor's office smells funny.

"Hello, Jane," a woman says from behind the counter. "You can bring Ms. Snow on back."

Jane grabs my hand. "Sure will." Her voice is super sweet and kind.

And completely fake. Just like her.

I pull my hand free and walk into the room by myself. I'm not a baby and I'm not scared of anything, and Jane better know that.

Another lady is waiting in the room. "Hello, Anna. I'm Nurse Kat. I'm going to be taking care of you. Can I ask you a few questions?"

Do I have a choice? Of course not; all the grownups want me to do what *they* want me to do, not what *I* want to do. And what *I* want is to not be here.

But this'll be quicker if I just do it and get it over with. If I fight it, it'll just drag it out longer.

"Do you remember receiving any vaccinations?" Nurse Kat wraps a black strap around my arm.

Just Another Door

"Is *this* a shot?" My heart pounds so loud I can hear it in my ears.

"No, sweetheart. This is to measure your blood pressure."

"I wasn't given a copy of her medical records," Jane says in that same fake voice. "We might as well get them done just in case."

Shots! No way. I want to run out of the office—but not with everyone watching me. I don't want people to think I'm afraid. I don't want *Jane* to see that I'm afraid of anything.

An old man comes in next with a file in his hands. "Hello, little lady. How about you tell me about the passing out you've been doing?"

He doesn't even look at me when he asks. He must not care what my answer is. Which is good because... what am I supposed to tell him? "I don't know. When I get... I mean when I feel..." I don't know what I'm supposed to say. "I... I'm not sure. I just... do."

"Did you have any kind of accident where you hit your head?" He looks at me.

There was this one time I fell off a horse and hit my head."

The doctor starts asking me all kinds of questions then. Suddenly, he doesn't care about his folder or click his pen. He wants more answers.

Jane says nothing. She just sits in the black chair, listening.

"Did you knock yourself out with the fall, like you fell asleep?" the doc asks.

"Yes, I did fall asleep. Then, when I woke up later, Thunder, the horse, was standing over me and nudging me with his nose. He was my friend."

"Well,, the good news is, we'll keep an eye on you. The only thing I can think is that you're passing out started after the injury."

"Yes, you are right. It started after I fell off Thunder."

"I think your head might still be healing from a concussion from that fall. Bad falls can take longer, and this sounds like a bad one." He looks at Jane. "If she starts to have more frequent episodes, let's get her back in. Let me check her out."

The doctor moves close. This is weird. I don't like men to stand this close to me. It reminds me of Roger standing in front of Jenna. I shiver.

"Kiddo, I need to look at your eyes, so follow the light."

I do as he says, but the bright light hurts my eyes.

"Everything looks good. I don't see any sign of a concussion or anything to worry about. She's all set to go."

I have no idea what he's talking about, but if I ask him, that might make me sound dumb, so I don't say anything. And, anyway, I just wanna get out of here before he remembers the shots.

I hop off the table and walk toward the door—

Just as Nurse Kat walks in with some needles—darn it. "We can make this quick, Anna. We'll do both at the same time."

I follow her directions and sit back down on the bed-looking thing. My heart pounds so hard it's hurting my chest because I was so close! I really don't wanna do this, but all of them aren't going to let me get out of here without getting the shots, so let's just get this over with.

The nurse and the doctor take a needle and stand on either side of me. "On the count of three," says the doctor. "One... two—"

"Ouch!" They jabbed me too early! "Where's the *three*?"

Everyone laughs, including Jane. "All done, sweetie. You're all set to go." Nurse Kat hands me a lollipop.

Is this supposed to make the pain better? It doesn't. I wish it did because I'd get a bag of them if it'd make *any* pain go away.

I hop down again. "Come on, Jane let's go." I swear she only took me to the doctors because she knew I'd get a shot.

* * *

This family only celebrates Christmas—not Halloween or Thanksgiving. Luckily, my teacher throws parties; otherwise, Jenna and I would miss out on the fun. The snow means Christmas is coming, and I know we'll celebrate because it's all my family talks about. Maybe that's why Marlene has left me alone—so she'll get lots of presents for Christmas.

Jane always tells Marlene now that she will return her presents if she starts any drama with me in class. Jane actually told her that my teacher could call the caseworker, who would put her in foster care along with Barry. It's been nice not hearing her voice annoying me in school. What Jane's doing is working.

"Yay. A school day off!" Jenna's shrill voice wakes me. I turn over, and there she is—watching the snow from the window. It's finally snowing! If it's gonna be a freezing December, we at least better get some snow.

The knock on the door makes both of us jump. "Morning, girls. It looks like a snow day for you." Jane wiggles her body all over. This is something weird she started doing when she seems happy. "I bet you both like that. Come downstairs. I have breakfast ready for you both." Jane closes the door behind her.

My foster mom has been surprisingly kind and helpful these past few weeks. She doesn't pay us much attention these days, well, unless she sends us to the basement. But it's all good now because when Jenna's in the cellar, I'm there for her and vice versa.

We still escape the dark basement for our fort. We stocked it with coloring books, crayons, and dolls that Jenna hid under her bed so Jane wouldn't throw them away. Plus, there were old toys in the bedroom that we didn't play with, so we took them to the fort. That was because of Jenna, not me.

"Anna, do you want to go outside to play in the snow?" Jenna's been so happy lately. I wonder if that's because Roger left us alone for the past few months. Maybe it's because I said I'd rat him out to Jane. He still gives us both the creeps when he watches us, but that's all--thankfully. He hasn't even tried to sit between us at the table.

And, it's helped Jenna a ton. She's gone back to her old self, laughing all the time. Me? I don't trust him and never will. If he can act like that in the past, he can do it in the future. It's weird how he just stopped, but I'm glad he did.

"Since you are out of school today, I thought it'd be nice to go for ice cream—*after* you clean your bedroom while I take this call."

Clean our bedroom? I've lived here for about three months now; she's asking us to clean our room now for the first time. Who did it for us before? I thought it was Jane. Why can't she keep doing it?

The phone rings from Jane's bedroom. She takes off in a hurry out of our room.

All of a sudden, Jane starts screaming at someone on the phone. We can hear her yelling all the way to our bedroom. That's not like her.

I run to the door so I can hear what's going on.

"Are you sure he was doing that? She's only sixteen years old. What proof is there? I don't believe it. Stop calling me." Jane slams the phone down.

Who the heck was Jane talking to? Was she talking about Roger doing something to a sixteen-year-old.

"Jenna, I think Jane was yelling about Roger, but I don't know for sure because—"

Jane shows up in our doorway. "I, um, need to spend the day with your father to talk with him about some things." Jane looks sad. "Can you please clean your room? We'll get ice cream later."

"Sure." We both say at the same time.

I wonder if she found out what Roger used to do to us—and might now be doing to a sixteen-year-old girl. Maybe *that's* why he's left us alone. If Roger is hurting another girl, I bet that it would make Jane sad to find out her husband is nasty and gross.

"Yay, ice cream!" Jenna claps.

My sister seems so happy that I don't think I want to tell her what I found out about Roger because I don't want to ruin her happiness.

We complete the room in a flash and are now on our way to ice cream—*without* Marlene. That's good but also strange because she's always with her mother. And Jane isn't talking much.

"Thank you, Jane, for taking us for ice cream."

"You're welcome, Anna." She doesn't say anything else on the ride.

"Mmm. Chocolate ice cream is my favorite." Jenna giggles as a piece of ice cream plops onto the ground. Then she whispers to me, "What's wrong with Jane?"

"I don't know." I feel bad about Jane. She's married to a monster, and she has no idea. Or, does she know?

The trip home is even quieter than the ride there. Jenna falls asleep in the backseat. And Jane's acting like she's in a trance and saying nothing at all.

We pull in behind Roger's truck, but Jane doesn't stop the car. She keeps getting closer, and closer, and then—*bang*! We hit the back of it.

Jenna pops up in the seat. "What was that?"

"Nothing to worry about. I got a little close to Daddy Rogers' car is all," Jane says, like it was an accident—which it wasn't. "Jenna, go upstairs and take a bath as soon as we get into the house."

My sister is always quick to follow directions, but that's still not true for me. I like to ask *why* my foster parents are asking me to do things—but today, I don't. Jane looks sad and mad. If she hit Roger's truck with her car, she's not messing around.

"Anna, I'd like to talk with you." Jane turns in the front seat to face me.

What the heck does she want to talk with me about? I always hate when she does this—when any of my foster moms do this—because it's usually something bad. Like, I'm in trouble or… I hafta leave.

"I had a teacher conference with your teacher yesterday."

Great, here comes the basement for me.

Jane lips raise on one side—her fake smile. "I'm glad to hear how well you're doing in school. Your teacher talks very highly of you."

"I love my teacher. Mrs. Swing is nice to me." My body is warm inside as I talk about her because I feel happy in class. Seeing her every day is the best.

"Well, I'm glad you are doing as well as you are in school. But, as for here… while things seem to be better, I'm wondering…" Jane rubs the temples on her head. "Anna, why won't you call me Momma Jane?"

Is this what's making her mad and it's not about Roger at all?

Why? She might be nicer to me lately, but I don't trust her. And she definitely doesn't need to know why or what I think.

But I hafta come up with something so I can make this stop. "Um… well… because… because you're *not* my mom."

She sighs.

I mean, I guess it hurts her feelings, but… it actually *is* the truth; she's *not* my mom. Momma Johnson was the closest thing I had to a mom, I guess, and Jane's nowhere close.

"Well, I guess you're right about that."

I can barely hear her. Why is she acting so different and sad? I don't *want* to hurt her feelings, but I can't lie, and I won't do something I don't want to do, like call her Momma Jane. I can't. "Can I go to my room and play?"

She rubs her head some more. "Yeah, get outta here."

I move as fast as I can. Jane is acting weird, and I don't want to be in the car if she decides to run into something else.

My room is empty. Where's Jenna?

I explore every inch of our bedroom, but… nothing.

I hear a noise coming from the bathroom. It sounds like someone's hurt or crying.

Jenna???

I run over and look through the keyhole—

Roger's putting his *thing* in Jenna's mouth!

Oh, hell no!

I bang on the door as hard as I can. "Jenna, it's me! Are you okay?" I turn the knob, but—

It's not turning. "Jenna!" I pound harder. Roger better stop!

"Anna!" he growls. "I'm helping Jenna with her bath. Go back to your room and it'll be your turn next."

"Okay, Roger, but I hafta call Jane up here 'cause the door seems to be stuck."

Yeah, he opens that door reeeeeeeeeeeeeeeaal quick. "Let me make this *very* clear, young lady." He shoves his shirt into his pants. "I'll get you moved out of this house sooner than you can blink an eye, and then I'll have your little foster sister here all to myself." He smiles like a sick clown, and I want to punch him.

Jenna bursts out of the bathroom, tears running down her face, and she bear-hugs me. "Please don't leave me, Anna!"

I glare at him. "If I catch you doing that to her again, I'll tell Jane."

He laughs at me. "No, you won't, because you know what'll happen. You'll be gone and this one will be *all* mine. "

"Roger, are you up there?" Jane interrupts us. Did she hear me talking?

"Yes, babe. I'll be right down." He pushes past Jenna and me, but stops before going down the stairs. "You can't stop me, Anna, if you want to save her."

I wanna shove him down those stairs, but... he's right. I can't do anything to him, or *I'll* be the one to leave.

But I have to stop him from hurting her.

I pull Jenna into our bedroom and slam the door shut. "Has Roger been doing that a lot to you?"

She wipes her tears. "Yes," she whispers so softly I almost can't hear her. "He told me that if I told you, he'll make you move." She tries to sniffle back some more tears, but that doesn't stop them. "I'm scared he'll make you go."

How can Jane *not* see what's happening? Doesn't she ever wonder why Roger's always upstairs when one of us is taking a bath? Doesn't she *know*? Or... maybe she *does*, but doesn't care...

Which makes her just as bad as Roger.

I lead Jenna over to her bed. "Let's come up with a code word. You can use it to tell me when Roger does something to you. No one will know what it means besides us." I wrap my arms around Jenna. My shirt's soaked with her tears.

She clears her throat. "Okay."

I squeeze her a little tighter. "How about snowflake? This way, you can say it anytime since it's winter and no one will know. It'll be like our little language. You can use it if you are afraid that Roger will do or *is* doing something to you."

"Great idea, Anna. I like that code word."

Jenna calms down a little. I don't know if snowflake will really work, but I know it might help Jenna feel better knowing she can talk to me in front of people without anyone knowing.

"Anna!" Jane shouts up the stairs. "Get yourself in that bathroom."

"Remember Jenna, *snowflake*."

Her mouth turns up in a smile but it's fake—I used to do the same thing after Derek and Scott did stuff to me... because if I didn't pretend I was okay, I wouldn't have *been* okay.

"Jenna, I know how you feel. Stuff happened to me, too. It's not your fault. You're just a kid. Roger's hurting you and making you believe that he'll have me moved if you don't do what he wants. It's okay to be sad and mad because it sucks what he's doing. You are also strong and, together, we are going to do something about this. We are *not* going to let this continue to happen. We won't."

I remember with Derek that I didn't fight him because I didn't want him to hurt my brother. My heart sinks and hurts like someone just sliced it open with a knife. What can I do?

I'm stumped. Damn it! I don't know... I don't know. Letting go of Jenna, I stand.

"I'm going to take my bath now. As soon as I leave, put the chair up against the door handle so Roger can't get in. If he tries, act dumb and scream for Jane to come help you with something."

Jenna follows me to the door. "What can I ask her to help me with? I'm already dressed."

"Good point." I look around for an idea—Jenna's hair's a mess.

"Don't comb your hair 'til I'm back. If Roger tries to come in, yell for Jane to help you with it."

"That's a great idea." She grabs the chair to shove under the handle after I leave.

I take a deep breath. At least I know she's safe, even if just for a short time.

Steam fills the air as I climb into the nice warm water. I wrap my arms around my legs and rest my head on my knees. Why do some men have to be so gross? Aren't there enough women in the world for them?

I turn my head and—

What the hell is that?

An… eyeball—? I forgot to place the towel over the keyhole. Urgh!

"Jane!" What? The HELL???!!! "Can you come up here, please, and bring me a towel?" I have no clue if there are towels or not, and I don't care. I just need to scare Roger away—

And… I hear footsteps running down the hall.

Good.

The creep. That's my new name for him.

A minute later, a knock makes me jump. He wouldn't… would he?

I'm not saying a word.

"Anna? It's me, Jane. Can I come in?"

This feels weird, but I called her up here, so I have to let her in. I don't want her to stop coming when I call. "Yup."

The door opens slowly. Jane looks toward the other side of the room as she puts the towels on the toilet, then she leaves in a hurry.

I'm glad she didn't watch me in the tub. Roger would have.

"Can you put the rest of the towels away for me in the closet when you're finished?" Jane asks from outside the bathroom. "I didn't want to invade your private time by doing it myself."

"Okay." That's the least I can do after she scared Roger off. I'm angry, though. How can she *not* know what her husband is doing to us? How?

The second the door clicks shut behind Jane, I scramble out of the tub and grab one of the towels and move to the side of the door, so Roger can't look through the keyhole at me.

My eyes are glued to the doorknob. *Please don't turn.* I don't want him to try to come in here.

I put my clothes on real slow while keeping an eye on that knob. I'll yell for Jane again if I have to.

I get everything back on, then open the door slowly.

The hallway's empty.

I run back into my bedroom. The door won't budge. I knock. "Jenna it's me." I whisper.

The doorknob rattles a little as Jenna moves the chair from the other side.

"Sorry Anna, I wanted to make sure Roger couldn't get in." Jenna heads back over to her bed.

"Good. I'm glad it worked but I have to tell you something." I pause catching my breath.

. "Guess who I saw looking through the keyhole of the bathroom door?"

"Roger?"

"Yeah, the creep. He was trying to see me naked." I exhale. "I know, let's put the laundry basket in front of the door when we take a bath, so it'll make noise if he tries to move it. And we have to remember to put a towel on the knob above the keyhole. I forgot to do it this time, and there he was.

"Let's do it. I don't like him watching me."

"Me neither." Him watching her *or* me.

"Time for bed, girls!" Jane calls up the stairs. "Lights off!"

Jenna puts the chair back under the doorknob like we've done every night since he was in our room.

We both say our prayers. I hope Jesus is happy that someone else is talking with him.

"Anna, are you excited about Christmas? Do you think Santa will come here next week?" She's happy talking about presents.

"I have no idea." That's the honest truth. I'm not sure if he'll show or not. He skipped my first foster home, though he did come to Sue's. "I hope so."

My old foster mother, Sue, gave me and my brother Curtis a huge Christmas. The first one I'd ever had. That's when I got Raggedy as a present. Thinking about Sue makes me sad because of what she did to me. But that Christmas with my brother Curtis was the best ever. That's what I want to think about—Christmas with my brother.

"Merry Christmas, Ms. Anna Snow. Your name is perfect for the holiday." Mrs. Swing is dressed up like Mrs. Claus when I get to class. "We have a lot of fun planned today. You wait and see."

My teacher has stuck to her word since she told Mrs. Alex about the basement, so maybe I *can* trust her now. Lately, when she says that she's going to do something, she always does it.

"Mornin', class! Have a seat. Let's start by checking out all the delicious food everyone brought."

Food? Awesome—but wait! Jane didn't give me anything to bring, so, I'm going to be the only one here with nothing. Just like the birthday party when, thankfully, my other nice teacher snuck in cupcakes she said were from my foster mother.

"Marlene," Mrs. Swing says, "please bring what you brought today to the front."

Ha! We live in the same house, so I won't be the only one with nothing.

"I sure will, Mrs. Swing. My mother made Christmas cupcakes for everyone."

What? She's lying. She has to be.

From under her desk, Marlene brings out this huge tray of white cupcakes with peppermint candy all over them.

Nope. She's not lying.

Why didn't Jane make something for me, too? Why just Marlene?

Jane must really hate me. But I thought she was starting to like me because she's been so nice lately.

I hate that no one loves me.

Marlene flings her hair as she walks back to her seat. The class is excited about the huge cupcakes and I'm just gonna look stupid.

"Anna, why don't you come up and grab the dessert you brought for class? I kept them on my desk for you."

Me…? What's she talking about?

I walk to her desk, and she passes me a huge tray of cookies in all different colors.

"Thank you, Anna," she says, "for bringing us such a big variety."

The class is quiet as I place them on the table, but then—cheers break out.

Whoa. They're *clapping* for me. I don't think I've ever been as happy in school as I am right this minute—and Mrs. Swing did that for me.

I glance at her and she winks. What a super cool teacher. Maybe I'll be a teacher and help kids someday.

Is she so nice because we are both foster kids? Or, rather, she *used* to be. But I guess you're always a foster kid at heart, even when you're older, right? Just like other kids come from their parents, Mrs. Swing and I are both from the same place. Foster care is our family.

"And our last student of the day—Mark. Can you come get the snack you left on my desk and take it over to the table, as well?" Mrs. Swing points in his direction,

Just Another Door

Huh? Mark doesn't have a clue what she's talking about—just like me.

Mrs. Swing hands him a bowl. "Here's the bowl of candy you made for everyone. Thank you, Mark."

Mark's smile is bigger than mine was... but, in my heart, I'm smiling even bigger because Mrs. Swing made sure every one of us has a snack on the table. She is really awesome!

"Okay, everyone, now for the best part."

I don't know anything that could be better than all these sweets on my desk. I can barely eat anything. Boy, how different things are now than when I lived with Mother and Daddy. Mother never gave me enough food for breakfast, forget about all these sweets.

If only Roger didn't live with Jane, this might not be such a bad place to stay.

"Kids, I asked your parents to have you bring in a gift that can be for a boy or girl. When I call you up one by one, put your gift under the tree in the corner."

We all look over. There are two presents under there already.

I have a feeling I know who they're supposedly from.

"As you can see," she says, "Anna and Mark have already put theirs under it."

This lady is really great.

"Anna," she says after everyone's put their gifts under the tree, "you're first since we're going to do this alphabetically, so lead us off."

Okay, so maybe she's not that great because, if she was, she'd know I don't like doing anything in front of the class.

"Look, everyone," Marlene says, "the dirtiest one goes first. It'll get better when she's done."

Mrs. Swing walks to Marlene's desk. "If I hear one more mean thing from your mouth, you will spend the rest of the class in the principal's office. Do I make myself clear?"

Everyone stops talking...

Marlene gulps, then nods.

Good. Serves her right. And now I can just get my gift and get out of here.

I grab the first gift I spot.

"Here, Anna. Come have a seat in this chair—" she slides one of the desk chairs to the middle of the room—"and open it. This way, everyone can see what you got."

Ugh. I really don't want everyone to watch me.

But I don't have a choice—I'll make a bigger scene arguing than by just opening this thing.

I sit on the chair and open the wrapping paper.

It's a box covered in butterflies and filled with pencils, crayons, and Christmas coloring books. This is the second-best gift ever because I *love* to color. Raggedy will always be my first best.

Each kid gets to pick a gift—and Marlene is last.

Mrs. Swing did that on purpose because Zoe went before Marlene.

I like that Marlene is getting punished for being mean to me. If only Jane could see it.

Marlene struts up front when Mrs. Swing calls her. "Saved the best for last, huh, teach?" She grabs a green box with a red ribbon.

It's cookies.

"I bring in a box of toys that cost my mother a lot of money and all I get is a small box of cookies?" She sticks out her tongue while she looks in the box. "I don't even like these."

Mrs. Swing shrugs. "Well, if you don't like your gift, you can leave them on the desk for everyone else to have." She reaches for the gift.

Marlene pulls the box to her chest. "Never mind. I'll give them to my dog."

We don't have a dog, so I know she's just being a snot. She's such a mean person. I can't imagine how the poor kid who brought in those cookies feels.

Well, given how she talks to me, I can.

I dunno… the fact that she got yelled at, had to pick last, and got a gift she doesn't like is kinda like an early Christmas present to me…

The end-of-day bell rings. "Okay, everyone," says Mrs. Swing, "have a nice Christmas. I'll see you in two weeks."

Two *weeks*? I won't see her for two weeks? All the other kids clap and cheer, but not me. Staying home for two weeks sounds like a nightmare.

I'm the last to leave the class on purpose. "Thank you, Mrs. Swing, for the cookies and the gift you did for me."

"Not a problem, Anna." She winks. "I remember what it was like being the only kid in class whose parent didn't send in a snack or a gift."

I leave class feeling normal—just like all the other kids—for the first time in a long time or… ever. *Thank you, Mrs. Swing.*

Jane meets me on the porch. Marlene's standing behind her. "Where the heck did you get those cookies?"

"Which cookies? Marlene's?"

Jane shakes her head. "No, not *those* cookies. The tray you took to class."

"Oh, Mrs. Swing brought them in for me to give out." I glare right back at Jane—and ignore Marlene.

"She did *what*?"

"Yeah. She did it for me and another kid. She also brought a gift in for us to give away in case our mothers didn't have money to do it or… forgot." I put that little pause in there on purpose because both Jane and I know she didn't *forget*. "Isn't she just the coolest teacher ever?" My smile spreads from ear to ear. I can't say the same thing about Jane's—hers turns into an ugly frown.

"Mom, it's not fair!" Marlene stamps her foot. "Her cookie tray was better than my cupcakes."

She's sooo right; mine *were* better than hers.

"If I wanted you to take in cookies, I would've made them for you. Since I'm *not* your mother, why would I do it? Isn't that what mothers do?"

Jane's niceness from the past weeks is gone. She's back to her old self. I knew it wouldn't last forever.

Jenna jumps in the middle of us all and hugs me. "I'm so glad you're home. Let's go play in our room."

Jane points to my boots. "Take them off before you head anywhere. I'll call you down for dinner."

As Jenna and I run upstairs, I hear Jane still trying to calm down her spoiled daughter. As soon as I get into the bedroom, I show Jenna my gift and tell her what Mrs. Swing did for me.

"That's so cool, Anna." She puts her head down. "I didn't bring a gift to class, so I couldn't get one."

Being in foster care sucks. I really wish I had a normal family, and we'd do normal things so I wouldn't have to worry about special classroom cookies and gifts.

"Don't worry, Jenna. I'll share mine with you."

"Anna?"

"Yeah?"

"You'll always be my sister, no matter what, right? Even if either of us moves? Can we be sisters forever?"

Dr. Sharon Zaffarese-Dippold

I look over at Jenna as she colors Santa's hat in my book. "Yes, we will Jenna. We'll be sisters forever."

After some time of coloring together, crayons still clutched in my hands, I jump up, my legs a tangled pretzel. "Gotta pee. I drank too much juice at school." As I waddle out of our bedroom, still hearing Jenna's echoing laughter, I can smell Jane cooking dinner. Phew. I finally made it, a wave of relief washing over me.

As soon as I get up from the toilet, the bathroom door swings open and in walks Roger. "What are you doing in here?" I snap at him.

He grins. "What do you think? I can do anything I want to you because you won't tell anyone. If you do, I'll get you kicked out of here." He steps closer to me.

Everything tells me to run, but he has the door blocked. "If you touch me, I'll tell Jane."

He steps closer. He smells all sweaty and gross as he grabs my neck. "No, you won't." He leans in and brushes his lips across mine.

I am *not* going to let him see how scared I am; bullies like to know you're scared of them.

"Christmas is coming, and you'll get shit. Or maybe…" His lips again touch mine for a second. "…you'll get a *real* kiss. And I bet you'll like it."

This can't be real.

He leans in quickly, and I lose my balance and jerk away from him.

I fall back against the wall.

Oh no. I'm pinned! I can't get around him! He's too big!

Stand up to him, Anna!

That voice in my head always helps me. I think it might be Jesus, because I always feel stronger when I hear it.

This time is just the same. I *am* stronger! "No, I won't *like* it!" And, without thinking, I lift my knee and *slam* it into his private area.

He yells and falls backward, grabbing his privates and groaning.

Good.

I get to my feet and run to the bathroom door. "If you touch me or Jenna ever again, I *will* tell Jane. And if you even *try* to have me moved, I'll tell your wife *everything*."

I run, my heart racing, to our bedroom, slam the door shut, then shove the chair under the knob.

"What happened, Anna?" Jenna asks. "What's the matter?"

Just Another Door

The matter is… Roger will *definitely* get me moved out of this house. How do I tell Jenna that I'm not gonna be able to protect her anymore?

But… I did find something that works against boys.

"Jenna, if Roger comes near you, you have to knee him in his privates so you can at least get away. If Roger starts walking funny, maybe Jane will finally notice what's going on."

Chapter 12
Snowflake

At dinner, Roger pretends everything is normal, but the intense glares he sends across the table says something else.

Until Barry spilled his drink all over the table.

"Uh oh. That's not good—and you want to be good because Santa's coming tomorrow!" Jane says, jokingly.

Barry's eyes start to tear up.

Poor kid. Though, honestly? I wouldn't mind spilled juice being the only thing I had to worry about.

Still, Barry doesn't know any better. I really hate when parents threaten kids with Santa to get them to behave. It wasn't like he did it on purpose. "Don't sweat it, Barry," I say. "Santa understands that accidents happen."

"Anna, you're right," Jane says as she fills Barry's glass again.

She's *agreeing* with me? *What* is going on with her? One day, she's a b-word and now she's back to being nice again. Jane's going crazy.

Or maybe... it's because she knows I'm going to leave.

Just Another Door

Jane and Roger ask Marlene and Barry what they want from Santa, but they completely ignore Jenna and me.

I don't want the both of us to sit there anymore and have to listen to this, so I ask her, "Wanna go upstairs to play patty-cake?"

"Sure do." She's as bummed about being left out as I am.

Once we're in our room and the door's shut, Jenna loses it. "Why didn't they ask *us* what we wanted? It's like we weren't even there." She wipes her face.

"I know, but let's do something fun so we don't have to think about it." I sit on the floor, my legs crossed.

She does the same, facing me, then she sweeps her messy blonde hair from her eyes, puts her hands up, and is prepared to play.

"Wait. We gotta figure out a plan first to stop Roger from hurting us."

Jenna nods, then drops her hands.

"Whatever we do, we hafta do it together. Roger wants to get us alone and we can't let that happen."

Jenna nods.

"If I need to pee, you're coming with me."

"Yup. And if I have to pee, Anna, you have to go with me, too. What about when we have to take a bath?" My sister looks up at the ceiling while asking the question.

"Well…, we'll do that together, too." I'd rather be alone in the bathroom, but Jenna's better than Roger. At least I know *she* won't want to hurt me.

"And, remember, Jenna—*snowflake,* if Roger tries anything…"

"Yeah. Snowflake."

We play patty-cake for a bit until my eyes feel like they're shutting whether I like it or not.

"I'm tired. I'm going to climb in my bunk."

My sister agrees.

I flop over onto my bed and glance down at her. "'Night, Jenna."

"'Night, Anna."

I position my pillow so it wraps around my head just like my blankets. It's something I do to be safe. I need it more than ever since I swear Roger was about to choke me.

Jesus, I'm going to talk with you in my head tonight because I don't want Jenna to hear me. Please keep Jenna and me safe from Roger. I know I shouldn't hurt him, but don't some people deserve it when you're trying to stick up for yourself? Roger deserved it. I'm sorry. I'm really sad and tired. I'll talk more tomorrow. 'Night, Jesus.

* * *

I've only ever liked one Christmas morning, so when Barry wakes us up, all excited, I just don't feel it. Jenna and I are the last ones to sit by the tree. Jane, Roger, Marlene, and Barry are wearing matching flannel pajamas, but Jenna and I sit here in shorts and a T-shirt. They keep this house so hot, we're sweating, and I can't imagine how those flannel pjs feel. That's so stupid to sit here in a hundred-degree heat just to wear a reindeer on their shirts.

"Okay, let's get this family Christmas started!" Jane says as she hands Marlene a big present wrapped in pretty paper. It has a pink ribbon—of *course*—that shimmers when the sunlight hits it.

Barry gets one next, then she gives one to Roger, and then he gives her one.

No one hands Jenna or I anything.

What?

They all dive in, unwrapping, while we... just sit there.

What kind of punishment is this?

Jenna grabs my hand when the second round of presents happen—again, with none for us.

This is just plain mean, and I'm about ready to say so when Jane *finally* hands us a package.

It's small and squishy and looks like we both get the same thing.

We rip the paper off—

Socks.

We each got a freakin' pack of *socks*. Who wants *socks* for Christmas? Santa did much better for me last year when I got Raggedy.

I set the socks on the floor. There has to be more. Maybe this was just like a joke or something because Barry and Marlene are getting a mound of presents, and they are *not* socks.

We keep waiting for more.

Jane walks to the back of the tree. "There are two presents left!"

Oh, good. These must be ours. I fidget around and squeeze Jenna's fingers. We're gonna have a great Christmas after all.

Jane picks up an enormous package. "Marlene, this is for you, sweetheart."

Marlene? Doesn't she have enough already, with a record player and an Easy-Bake oven in her pile? Now she's got a giant dollhouse?

What the hell?

Jane holds up the last present. "And this is for…" She spins from one kid, to the next to the next, the smile on her face making me think we just might have a chance.

I don't care if I have to share it with Jenna; I just want something other than stupid socks.

But then she tosses the present to Barry.

That's *it*? We get *one* freakin' present and it's *socks*?

Jenna and I just look at each other. Yeah, we're outta here.

We go up to our room. Jenna flies onto her bed and cries into her pillow.

I wanna do that, too, but I don't want her to keep being sad, so I sit on her bed and pat her back.

She takes a couple of deep breaths, then rolls over. "Why do we have to be foster kids? Why can't we have a normal family like everyone else? Why, Anna?" Her voice cracks.

"I know, Jenna. The socks suck. I don't even like white. I'd rather wear bright green."

A fit of giggles overcomes Jenna, and I can't help but laugh along. "Who needs Jane's stupid present, anyway? Mrs. Swing got me a great gift, so let's play with it. That'll show Jane. Let's have fun together, no matter what they try to do to us. We have each other, Jenna." I stand up.

"Yeah, that'll show her. You're the best Christmas gift ever, Anna." Jenna gets off the bed after me.

Now, I'm the one hugging her. "So are you, Jenna."

I feel like crying, but I won't. Jenna just stopped herself, and I don't want to make her feel bad again.

Suck it up, Anna.

I pull out the coloring books and box of crayons. I'm so glad Mrs. Swing thought about doing this. At least I have one grownup in my life who cares about me—and I am counting down the minutes until this break is finally over. Then, I can go back to school and see one of my favorite people, Mrs. Swing. I like myself when I'm around her. I feel smart and people like me.

Dr. Sharon Zaffarese-Dippold

"Girls, come down for Christmas dinner now, please!" Jane yells up the stairs.

Spaghetti. Jane's favorite thing to cook. We have it all the time.

Tonight is different, though. Marlene is sitting on her mother's lap. This is so weird. I scrunch my face together.

"Whatcha looking at?" Marlene snaps at me.

"Nothing. I'm looking at nothing."

"Mom, wanna play checkers with Dad and me while we eat?" Marlene talks like a baby while she jumps off Jane's lap to go get her gift.

Ugh. This is so gross. I don't wanna watch them act all lovey-dovey. Everyone talks about what they got for gifts while Jenna and I eat quietly.

Roger is back to sitting in between us. Vomit would taste better than the spaghetti on my plate.

Something is on my leg. "Jane, I think something is crawling up my leg. Could it be a bug? Could it be a rat in the house that's under the table?" I bend down to look. I know it was Roger trying to run his hand up my leg, but I want to make him uncomfortable.

"Here's the game." Marlene sits her checkerboard up in front of her father, creepy Roger.

I place my fork on the table with the sharp end facing up. "Roger, do you think it was a rat or something?"

Sitting this close to him makes every part of my body feel like it's on edge. Like I'm standing on the side of a cliff and am trying to keep my balance.

I stare at Roger, holding my fork. "Did you have anything crawling up your leg, Roger? How about you Jenna? Did you feel something crawling up yours?"

"Yeah, Anna, just before you did."

"You *didn't* feel it, Roger? Jenna and I did. How strange." I don't blink as I stare at his face.

"Um... I don't know what you girls are talking about."

Of course he'd say that.

"Girls, knock it off. I'm sure it was nothing." Jane stares at Roger while she talks to us.

"I'm not hungry," I say. "Can we go, Jane?"

"No, Anna. You sit here 'til we are done. Jenna, it's your turn to clean up today when we're finished."

Oh, I see how it is: no presents for foster kids and make them clean up from dinner and Christmas so you can act all happy with your real family. Of *course*, she asked Jenna to clean up because her lazy ass won't.

Jenna heads into the kitchen.

Roger stands up. "I'm going to get a drink. Does anyone want something?"

Jane shakes her head. "No, honey. Thank you for asking, though." She winks at him.

She wouldn't do that if she ever found out that her *honey* likes little girls better than her.

"Mom, you're cheat—"

"Snowflake, snowflake, snowflake!" comes from the kitchen.

Oh no! Roger's in there!

I jump out of my seat, banging the chair into the table leg.

"Where the hell are you going in such a hurry?" Jane snaps.

To stop your husband from doing gross things to my sister... "I, uh, forgot to tell Jenna something. I'll be right back."

But Jenna's not in the kitchen.

I spin around—where *are* they?

And then I hear a sound that reminds me of when Mama Cat had her kittens coming from the basement.

There!

I shove the door open and—yeah, Roger's hand is on parts of Jenna's body that it shouldn't be, and he's got her pinned against the wall.

His other hand is around her neck—just like he did to me.

"Stop!" I yell as I run down the stairs.

"Anna, what are you yelling at?" Jane hollers from the dining room.

I don't have time to answer her. I have to get Roger off Jenna.

I knock his arm off her. "I warned you, Roger, that I'd tell Jane everything if you ever touched either of us again." I pull Jenna toward me. "Time to go, Jenna." I lead her up the stairs, then back into the kitchen... on my way to the dining room.

He's *not* getting away with this. He's *not* going to touch her or me ever again. "Jane!" I yell. "I need to talk to you!"

Roger grabs my wrist and yanks me around. "Don't. You. Dare."

"Watch. Me." I give him the same attitude right back because he's not gonna scare me. What he was doing is gross and wrong, and I'm tired of letting him get away with it.

I yank my arm away and head into the dining room. "Jenna and I have something to tell you." I pull out a chair for Jenna and me to sit, facing Jane. Thank goodness she's the only one left at the table.

Jane looks back and forth between us. "What's going on? You two look like you've seen a ghost or something."

More like a troll—Who waltzes in at that very moment with a drink in his hand.

He stands next to Jane. "Would you like a chug of this soda?" he asks, as if everything's okay.

Everything is *not* okay. I want to wipe that stupid grin right off his face.

"No, thanks. I need to find out what the heck is up with the girls."

Jenna grabs my leg under the table.

I squeeze her back gently. We have to do this. "I have to tell you that Roger's been…"

Roger raises the soda.

He's challenging me.

He shouldn't do that. I don't turn down challenges. And I usually win 'em.

I take a deep breath and lift my chin. "Roger has been… um…" saying these words is harder than I'd thought because once I say them, they're real. I can't take them back. "He's been…"

Do I really have to say it to her? Can't she tell what I'm trying to tell her? Why do *I* have to be the one to say the horrible disgusting things he chooses to do?

It's not fair. None of this is fair. Not us being foster kids or having to change houses or not getting Christmas presents and, most especially, not feeling safe in the house we're living in. There's always a Derek or a Sue or a Scott and now a Roger. Why?

"Anna, what's going on here?" Jane finally says something.

"Roger's been touching both me and Jenna. He kisses us and comes into the bathroom while we're bathing. He touched Jenna's girl parts and even put his *thing* in her mouth. He even tried to choke us!"

I say it all without crying or screaming, but I say it. It's done. I actually *did* it. I spilled my guts to someone.

"What?" Roger acts like he's so surprised—and maybe he is because I actually told her. "She's lying, Jane. Anna's just ticked off that I told her she'll be in the basement because she cussed me out in the kitchen. She's just trying to start a fight by lying. You know how these foster kids can be. They're a bunch of liars." He runs his skeevy hand on her arm.

I want to puke.

Jane, though... She... She kinda goes stiff. Frozen. She's just sitting there, blinking, but I don't think she's looking at anything.

Did she hear me?

Roger fidgets with his hair while he slides a chair out from the table to sit next to her. He leans over with his mouth close to her face. "Honey, can you believe she's trying to accuse me of something so awful?"

Jane still doesn't move a muscle.

What the heck is going on?

I squeeze Jenna's leg again. The truth is out. Jane *has* to do something about it. She *has to* believe me. Believe *us*.

Finally, she turns her head in my direction, and her eyes are squinting so tight, I don't know if she can even see me.

"Well, *maybe*, Anna, you girls shouldn't wear such short shorts around the house."

What?

And then she just... leaves the room.

What?

Roger follows her, but shoots me a grin so evil, I don't even know what to say.

What the *hell* just happened? Does she really think our *shorts* are the reason Roger is doing this to us?

I don't get it. I don't understand a single freakin' thing. She is blaming our *shorts*—this house is a freaking oven and her damn daughter wears shorts; why is it *our* fault that Roger does terrible things to us?

Jenna grabs my hand. "Do you... Do you think he's gonna come in our room tonight to hurt us?"

My movements are slow as I stand up from the table. It's like my mind is moving, but my body is having a tough time following. "Let's make a plan. If Roger's coming for us, we need a way to escape. Let's run upstairs, grab some warm clothes, a pillow, and a blanket, then head to the basement!" Just like in my last foster home when I hid from Scott in the beating room. People don't expect you to hide in places they think you're afraid of. "Roger will never think to look for us down there. And if he does, we'll hear him and can escape out the metal doors."

"But it's freezing down there," Jenna says, shivering.

"I know. We just gotta put on a lot of clothes and grab our blankets. C'mon. Let's go now while Jane's yelling at him." I wish I could hear what she's saying, but I don't want to be close to Roger anymore.

Jane's words are easier to hear as we tiptoe into our bedroom to get warmer clothes and blankets.

"What if they tell someone, Roger? We could lose Marlene and Barry."

Jane's worried about *Marlene and Barry*? She's not upset that her husband likes to hurt little girls? What is *wrong* with foster care parents?

Jenna and I may have to come up with a plan to run away because it looks like Jane isn't gonna stop him. But it's freezing out; where are we supposed to go?

I'll think about it later because we hafta get dressed warm. We throw on sweats and sweatshirts, then grab every blanket we own.

Tiptoeing, we head downstairs, then into the basement. Jenna's right—it is freezing! Holy crap!

We huddle against the blue door, then dig in the cold soil until we find the flashlight. Now we have light and can see the frost on the windows.

"Let's go sit by the furnace to warm up," I whisper as I stand up with the light.

"Okay." She helps me make a blanket fort.

"What do you think is gonna happen to us tomorrow?"

That's a really good question—and I have no clue what to tell her. The thought of being moved, of leaving her alone with Roger, makes me worry so much that my stomach hurts. If only I had let him kiss me—

No. I couldn't. It was too gross. I can still feel his stinky breath on my face. Maybe it would've been the right thing to do to protect Jenna, but what about me?

"It's so cold, Anna."

Yeah, me, too—inside and out.

But I'm okay for now. I'll worry about tomorrow when it gets here.

I wrap my arms around Jenna and hug her tighter. "In my first foster home, Jenna, I learned a trick when I was cold at night. I would take the sheet over my head and then breathe under it. My breath warmed me up. Let's try it."

It helps. At least we won't freeze to death tonight.

I don't know what we're gonna do about all the other nights we're gonna have to be down here, though.

* * *

The heavy stomps jolt us from sleep. I have no clue what time it is, but we can hear people talking. I nudge Jenna. We haven't taken the blanket off yet. "We have to go. It's morning."

Jenna wipes her eyes. "What time is it?" Her voice is scratchy.

"I have no idea except that it's morning because the sun's out." I point to the light in the small window that is covered in ice on the inside.

"We better get going. We can stop at the top of the stairs and wait for it to be clear before we come out."

Jenna nods.

The kitchen's clear. We open the door and stand by the sink. "Let's act like we've been here all morning if someone comes in."

"Sounds good, Anna."

I pretend to get a drink, grabbing a glass and filling it with water.

Jane runs into the room. "Where have you girls been? Never mind. I need you to follow me."

Jenna and I look at each other. "She didn't say anything about Roger."

"I dunno."

We hold hands as we walk into the dining ro—Mrs. Alex's here.

I'm being moved again.

But, wait. Next to my garbage bag by the front door is... *another* one. "Is Jenna coming, *too*?"

"Yes, now get your bags and let's go," says Mrs. Alex

I can't get out of this house fast enough—especially since Jenna's coming with me. I grab my garbage bag and drag it out the door.

I'm even happy to climb into the backseat of the green monster. "C'mon, Jenna, hop in." We pile our bags onto the seat next to us.

It's nice having someone else in the back seat with me, and, if it can't be Curtis, I'm glad it's Jenna.

Mrs. Alex closes my door. "You guys look crowded back there with your stuff. Does anyone want to ride up front?"

"Nope," we both say at the same time.

Mrs. Alex turns the car on, then looks at us in the mirror. "What on earth did you two girls do to this family? I got an emergency call at midnight to pick you up first thing this morning."

I could tell her what *Roger* did, but she's not gonna believe me. She never does. But, this time, I don't care—we're outta there *and* I have Jenna with me! I hope we get to stay at this new house together. "Is Mrs. Alex your social worker, Jenna?"

"No, I'm not her caseworker," Mrs. Alex says as she turns around to look to back out of the driveway. "*Her* worker is on vacation, so I'm filling in for this crisis move."

"What's a crisis move, Mrs. Alex?"

"It means that we had to move you in a hurry, so it's called a crisis. I'm taking you to an emergency home. You won't be there long, just long enough to find foster homes for you both."

Well, at least we're together now.

It's not long before Mrs. Alex drives up to a beige house with black shutters.

"This looks like a nice place," I say.

"Oh, the Zells are very nice people. You'll stay here just long enough for the county to find a longer placement for you."

A short woman with beautiful skin opens the door when Mrs. Alex knocks.

She shakes Mrs. Alex's hand and then mine when I stick it out.

"Hello. I'm Anna Snow."

Chapter 13
Officer Joe

"Welcome, Ms. Anna Snow. I think your name is beautiful. You're welcome to call me Ms. Liz—Liz, if you like."

Finally, someone who gets that foster kids don't always want to call these helping people *Mom* or *Dad.* They should be called *Foster* and their name. Like *Foster Deb* or *Foster Jim.* But not *Mom* or *Dad.*

And it ought to be the foster kids who make the decision about what to call them.

She leans in. "Are you okay?"

Am I okay? What a big question. How could I be? I've moved a zillion times and stand at just another door into a new world that I have no clue on how it works. Am I okay? "Yeah, I'm good," I lie. But what can she or anyone do to help me? What's the point? No one's in this world with me, except for Jenna, and that's just for a short time. I've accepted that fosters can't do anything to help except offer me a place to live.

"Hello, Ms. Liz. I'm Jenna."

The nice lady shakes her hand. "Why do you carry garbage bags with you?"

Jenna shrugs.

"Because that's what foster care makes us put our stuff in when we move," I say.

Ms. Liz looks at me with kind eyes. "We'll have to fix that, won't we?" Ms. Liz giggles. "Do you have anything else?"

My foster sister quickly says no.

But I say, "Yes, I do, I have to go get—"

Oh no.

My body is building up with something that starts at my toes. It's not the passing-out thing, but something different. My heart races so fast, I can't breathe.

"Are you okay, Anna?" Ms. Liz looks worried. "Girl, you lost all your color in a second."

"I can't breathe. I can't—"

Mrs. Alex jumps in front of me. "Are you okay, Anna?" Her eyes are enormous.

"No! I'm not okay! I forgot Raggedy and Teddy!" I gasp for air, bending over. "I. Um. Left them at Jane's house." Tears are falling and I can't stop them. And I don't care if people are all around me. "Please, please, please, Mrs. Alex, can you go get them before Jane throws them away? Please." I beg with everything I have in me.

A man comes out of the house. "What's going on?" This man is enormous with big muscles.

"Um. Um. I left my friends at the last foster home." I don't like men, but he asked and I'm going to tell him.

"Calm down, child. Mrs. Alex will make sure she gets them this week for you."

"No. No. You don't understand. Jane will throw them away. She *will*." My voice is hoarse from crying. I cover my head with my hands and sob. How could I forget them? I was so excited about Jenna coming with me that I forgot my stuffed animal friends, Teddy, and my doll, Raggedy.

"Can you go today, Mrs. Alex, and pick up her stuff? Clearly, it's bothering her." The man points at me.

"I wish I could, but I have another appointment. I can call the family today, though, and ask them to store Anna's stuff until I can get there later this week to pick them up."

She's crazy. Is she not listening? Jane will throw them out.

"No!" My voice is loud enough for everyone to hear me in this neighborhood. "Jane will throw them away! Please! Please!"

Mrs. Alex puts her hand on my shoulder. "Calm down, Anna. I'm not able to go today. I'm sure—"

Wrenching myself free from my caseworker's grasp, I tumble to the hard ground. I double over, my body collapsing into a ball, a silent scream ready to break out. With each sob, my chest heaves and tears flood my face like a river. My heart's being ripped out. My body shakes all over as I cry. *I'm sorry, Raggedy. I'm sorry Teddy. I'm so sorry.*

"This is crap. You can see how upset the little lady is. I'll go get them myself." The giant man walks back into the house, then comes back out with his car keys in hand. "Come on, little lady, come with me. Let's go get your stuff."

He doesn't have to ask me twice. I jump up and run to hug him. My arms don't fit around him, but I squeeze as much as I can. "Thank you. Thank you."

He squeezes me back—but not a creepy squeeze like Roger's. Kinda like the bear hugs I got from my first foster dad.

"Excuse me, Mr. Zell. Anna may *not* go back to a foster home that we moved her from."

We both glare at Mrs. Alex.

"That's a stupid-ass rule if I've ever heard one and I don't care about policies that hurt children. We *are* going after her stuff since you don't have time to help her. Might be something you want to bring up with your organization. Clearly, I'm a police officer and not a threat to this child. So, unless you think you can stop me, we're leaving." He puts his arm around my shoulder. "Let's go, Anna."

Turning around, I see his police car. I didn't even notice it before. "We're going in *that*?"

"Yes, we are."

"Can I come, too?" Jenna hollers.

Mr. Zell spins around to face my foster sister. "Of course. Let's move along."

Jenna runs fast to stand with us.

Mrs. Alex walks in our direction, talking.

I have no idea what she's saying because I can't hear her. I also don't care. I just want my stuffed friends.

Mrs. Alex yells at Mr. Zell when she gets close to the police car.

"Officer Zell,. they can*not* go into the home. Can they wait in the car while you get their stuff and then Anna can confirm if it's everything?" Mrs. Alex looks like the one begging now.

Mr. Zell looks out the passenger window at my caseworker. With a smile, he says, "Sounds like an excellent compromise," then rolls up the window and starts the car. "Watch this, girls. It shows that we mean business."

The sound and the lights make Jenna and I jump. It's kinda weird sitting in a cage. I feel like a puppy in a pound.

After a few seconds of driving, Mr. Zell turns off the lights and alarm, picks up this walkie-talkie-kinda thing and talks to someone. "We're heading to Roger and Jane Tart's house."

"The kids came from that home?" the voice on the other end says. "I'm sure they didn't have an easy time there. We've been watching that family for a little while, as some girls who lived there before came forward with some interesting things." My new foster father puts the talkie on his leg, making it harder for me to hear.

"Yes, I have these two little ladies in the back seat, and we are on a stuffed animal recovery mission. Is the station empty? I might swing by and give them a tour since I need to finish a minor detail on a report from yesterday. Is Officer Cunningham around?"

"Yup, she's working the desk today," the voice tells him.

"Great. She can keep them entertained as I finish the report. Is Forest back in or still out on the beat?"

"He's here," the voice replies.

"Great, bud. See you soon." Mr. Zell has a deep voice.

"Okay, Chief. Out."

He called Mr. Zell *Chief*. I wrap my finger through the cage fence behind Mr. Zell. "Are you a Native American?"

He chuckles. "You heard that conversation, huh?" He smiles in the mirror at us. "No, I'm not Native American. He calls me *Chief* because I'm the chief of police and oversee a few precincts."

The radio makes a noise and then there's a voice. "Hey, Chief. Notified the foster home. They know you're coming and will have the kids' items ready to go."

"Thanks." Mr. Zell puts the talkie away, then grabs his police hat and puts it on his head. His jacket is on the passenger seat. "We're almost at the foster home, girls. I want the two of you to stay in the car. Don't

Just Another Door

get scared if you try to get out. The back doors are locked and can only be open from the outside. I won't be in the home long."

Just as he tells us this, we pull into Jane and Roger's driveway.

Jenna sinks back into the seat—I swear she's shaking. "Jenna, are you okay? We don't have to go in."

Mr. Zell turns around with a concerned look. "Are you afraid, Ms. Jenna?"

She pushes further back into the seat at the same time she nods.

"Don't worry, little lady, I won't let either of them approach the police car." He slides on his police jacket and buttons it up as he opens his door.

I wrap my arms around Jenna. "We're okay right now. Roger can't hurt us anymore."

Mr. Zell looks at us through his door window. "*No* one can hurt you. You're safe with Liz and me. I'll be right back."

We watch the back of our new foster father walk to the nightmare house we just came from and it hits me—I won't see Mrs. Swing again or Marie. I'm sad. Will this ever get easier? Maybe, I just need to think about other things instead of being sad, like hoping foster homes have certain things, like a horse. If I think about that, being sad will go away.

'Bye, Mrs. Swing. You were the BEST teacher I've ever had. I hope, someday, I can come back and visit you. Thank you. Goodbye, Marie. Thank you for being my friend and sticking up for me.

My body hurts. It's like it's crying all over. I keep losing the people I care about.

"Wanna play patty-cake while we wait?" Jenna's voice breaks my thoughts.

Within a short time, we see Mr. Zell leaving the house carrying a garbage bag.

Jane is walking next to him. I'm sure she's using her sweet voice. She waves at us both.

Jenna and I do the same thing—nothing.

Mr. Zell stops midway and pulls out Raggedy and Teddy from the garbage bag. What's he doing?

He tucks both of them under his arm, then gives the garbage bag back to Jane. He tips his hat to her, then turns toward us, leaving her standing alone.

Goodbye, tree fort. Goodbye, kitty. I hope you found a house. And goodbye, Barry. I hope you'll be safe living with this family.

Dr. Sharon Zaffarese-Dippold

My door opens.

Raggedy and Teddy! "Thank you, Mr. Zell. Thank you." I'm so, so happy.

"You can call me Joseph, Joe, or whatever you like." He smiles and shuts the door.

Happy tears fall on my friends as I hug them. "I'm so sorry I forgot you both. I won't ever do that again."

"Can I hold one, Anna?" Jenna doesn't have any friends like this; she has nothing but clothes.

I hand her my doll. "You can hold Raggedy. She'll help you feel better."

Jenna squeezes her tightly.

I do the same with Teddy.

Officer Zell—um, Joe pulls into a place that's not his house. "I need to stop here for about ten minutes. I'll give you ladies a tour of the barracks."

Whatever that means. Should we go into a place we don't know?

Well… why not? I did it before when I jumped onto a school bus that took me to church. My life changed because of that—I met Jesus and I've had him as a friend ever since. This could be a good thing.

"Hello, Chief," says a woman with blonde hair as soon as we walk in. "Who are these little ladies?" She comes out from behind the tall desk and gives Jenna and me a big lollipop with all different colors on it.

"'Morning, Officer Cunningham. I'd like you to meet Jenna Storm and Anna Snow."

The lady holds out her hand for Jenna and me to shake. "Nice to meet you both, SnowStorm."

How did she know that's what we call ourselves?

Joe talks to another officer when the guy walks through the door, and they even *high-five* like Jenna and I do. "Officer Forest, can I grab a minute of your time to follow up on our conversation earlier about the foster family we've been talking about?"

"Sure, Chief."

I wonder if Mr. Zell—Joe—is going to talk to him about those other girls from Jane and Roger's. I know he didn't want me to hear that because he turned his walkie-talkie off right away, but we've lived there; I can't ever forget it and I bet those other girls won't either.

"Girls, I'll be right back. Enjoy the tour with Officer Cunningham." Mr. Zell then disappears into a room with Officer Forest.

Just Another Door

"Come on, SnowStorm! This way!" Officer Cunningham waves her arm over her head as she turns like the leader of a parade. She then grabs some plastic badge-thingies off a wall and hands them to us. "Put these on as official tour badges! Welcome to the being junior officers!"

We pin the badges on our clothes. I wish this thing could keep me safe from *any*thing—especially men who're into young girls and foster mothers who're mean.

"This is called a cell. It's where we keep bad men and women. Do you want to go in?"

"Yes." Jenna runs in without me.

I step into the small room. I can't imagine spending my life in jail and only living in this space. "Officer Cunningham?"

"Yes, Officer Snow?"

I giggle at my new name. "Do men who hurt little girls go to jail and have to live in this room?"

Officer Cunningham's smile disappears. "Yes, Officer Snow, they do." She stops talking and looks at Jenna and me. "Has anyone hurt you two?"

What do we say to that? We can't tell the truth—besides no one ever believing me, what if Roger knows where we live and comes to hurt us?

I look at the floor. "No, I was just curious is all."

"Yeah, we were just curious." Jenna says a little louder than me.

"Well, you know... if anyone has ever hurt you, you can tell a police officer, and they will keep you safe."

I doubt that. No one's kept me safe so far. Worse yet is when I tell someone—things always get worse for me.

"We'll remember that, thank you." I grab Jenna's hand and pull her out of the cell.

Officer Cunnungham takes us everywhere, including the lunchroom. "Let's head out to the main office and see if the Chief is ready to go."

Mr. Zell is waiting for us by the time we get there. "Let's get going, girls. I'm sure Liz is wondering where I've taken you."

Jenna runs over to hug Officer Cunningham. "I'm going to be a cop like you when I grow up."

In no time, we are back at the house. I love this house; I'm a sucker for black, and this place has black shutters, a black garage door, and a black front door with a pretty purple wreath!

Dr. Sharon Zaffarese-Dippold

As soon as the car stops, I take Raggedy from Jenna. "I'll give her back when we go to bed if you like, but I have to be the one to walk her in, so I don't ever forget her again. If I carry her, then I know where she is."

Liz meets us at the door. "Welcome back, young ladies. I've made some grilled cheese sandwiches in case you're hungry."

"I'm starving!" I say.

"Me, too!" Jenna replies and we both run to the table. A sandwich, chips, and a drink are sitting in two places.

Liz makes a *great* sandwich. This is so much better than Jane's. This home might be okay because the first thing this foster mother did was feed us. That's a good sign.

"Do you girls have any questions for us?" Liz and Joe sit at the table with us.

I have never had a foster parent ask me this—like... like they care what I want. Wow! I mean, I've always wanted someone to ask, but to actually have them do that... It's weird. But in a nice way.

As if what I want... matters.

As if *I* matter.

I'm shocked that I now have a choice.

"Um, yeah. I have a question." I sit up straighter. This is a really important question. "Do you have a horse?" That would make this place *perfect*.

Liz smiles. "I wish we did, Anna. Our property isn't big enough for one. But I *know* someone who has horses. Maybe we can plan a visit."

"That would be so awesome, Mrs. Zell!" I try to be polite like Jessica, my old foster mother, taught me. If people are polite to me, then I will be polite to them. If people are mean, then I'm going to mean back.

"Sweet girl, you can call me Elizabeth, Liz, or whatever you like, *except* Mrs. Zell. That makes me feel like I'm my mother-in-law." She chuckles. "Now, when you're done eating, I'll show you all the food cupboards so you can help yourself when you're hungry."

"Help ourselves? To *food*?" I glance at Jenna. Did I hear her right?

"Yes, of course, to food—well, just the snacks. There's no need for you to cook, because I'll do that."

Joe bumps her shoulder. "She's a superb cook, too. Wait'll you taste it!" Joe seems super nice to Liz. He kisses her cheek—and doesn't act creepy at all. "I'll show the girls to their room while you clean up from lunch."

We go up four stairs and then another set goes downstairs from the kitchen. Joe takes us that way and shows us two rooms that have bunk beds in both. Everything looks so clean. Jane's house was clean, too, but it felt dark. This house has a lot of pretty colors on the walls.

"You can choose to sleep together or separate, whichever is more comfortable for you."

I hope Jenna wants to keep sleeping together—I mean; I know everything *seems* wonderful, but I've learned that things—and people—can change fast in foster care.

"Each room has its own bathroom with everything in it you need, including new toothbrushes. When you want to lock the door, just push the button on the knob. And it's all yours; no one else will be using this bathroom."

This place almost seems too good to be real.

"I'll give you some time together so you can decide who will sleep where. Go ahead and check out the room, then come on back upstairs when you're done."

He leaves, and Jenna and I explore our new room.

"Whoa, Anna! Come see this!" She's pointing to a large TV on the dresser. "Is this for us?"

Us? I hope that means she wants to sleep in here with me. "I think it is, Jenna... *if* we're sharing the room."

"Of course we are! I don't want to sleep alone—do... you...?"

"No way!"

We high-five. We're foster sisters through thick-and-thin!

We choose the bedroom with the white bunk beds that have giant purple fluffy blankets and big white pillows.

Jenna jumps onto the bottom bunk.

"Hey, Jenna, I know Jane didn't want you to sleep on the top, but we're not with Jane. If you want the top, you can have it. Do you?"

She jumps up fast, standing on the bottom bunk to peer at the top one.

After a few seconds, she jumps down. "Thanks, but I'll keep the same bed just like we had." She dives back into her bed. "It's so comfortable. Wait 'til you feel it."

Mmmm. My foster sister is right.

Our new foster mother knocks on the door. "Girls? Can I come in?"

"Sure!" Jenna says, practically bouncing on the bottom bunk.

Dr. Sharon Zaffarese-Dippold

I don't know that I've ever seen Jenna this happy.

Liz pops her head around the door. "Can you both come to the kitchen area so Joe and I can talk with you? We like to have family meetings."

Uh oh—I've heard that before. Now we get all the rules and what we can and can't do. They made us all happy with the room and our own bathroom and now we're gonna find out all the bad stuff.

Why can't any home be just good and not have the bad?

Chapter 14
Cupcakes

Liz and Joe sit opposite me and Jenna at the kitchen table, and she touches Joe's hand. "We'd like to talk to you about your stay with us. We want to make sure you understand everything, so nothing comes as a shock to you."

A shock. What more can be a shock than my life? Never knowing when or where I'm moving or who I'm going to be forced to live with? Wondering what they'll do to me. *Those* things are a shock.

Liz taps the table. "Can you hear me, Anna? You look like you're somewhere else in your head?"

She has a point—I do that a lot. Mainly because it's safe in my head. Safer than in some of the houses I've been in. "Um, yeah, I hear you."

"We want to be sure you understand that your stay with us is temporary. We are an emergency placement for kids who need to get out of one foster home before another one becomes available. Liz frowns.

"You're saying we're not gonna be here long?"

Liz's face changes and she looks a sad dog.

Joe holds her hand. "You're right, Ms. Anna. We aren't ready yet to be full-time foster parents. My work schedule needs to change a little for me to be around more, but that's not an option yet."

Yeah, I get it; we're gonna get shipped out soon. The *one* nice place and it's not gonna be for long. Story of my life... "So why are you even taking kids in the first place?"

Liz takes a big breath. "We want to do the best for as many kids as we can."

"Why don't you have your own kids?" I mean, he *seems* like he loves her and that he's a good guy, and they like kids so...?

Joe clears his throat. "Some couples can have children, and some are not so lucky. Liz and I are not able to have our own children." Joe kisses the back of Liz's hand.

Well, *that's* horrible. I mean, these people seem super nice and would be great parents, but they can't have any. My birth mother Norma is a horrible mother and couldn't keep me—but she could have kids. It seems that bad things don't happen to just good *kids*; good grownups can have bad things happen to them. That doesn't seem fair. But, then, if there's one thing I've learned in my time in foster care, it's that there are many things in life that aren't fair.

"Your stay with us will only be about a week because they're looking for new foster homes for you both. We'll tell you everything, so you'll know what's happening and not be surprised when it's your time to leave us." Liz talks softly and looks down. Is she sad?

If she is, why don't they just keep us here?

"Do you think they'll let us stick together? "Jenna asks.

Joe leans his elbow onto the table. "I hope so. You two seem close."

"We are. We became sisters." Jenna smiles, showing all of her teeth—something new for her because I've never seen her this happy and relaxed.

"Can we talk about school?" Liz glances between Jenna and me.

"Ugh. Now I have to start all over again at a new school," I mumble. That's almost as bad as starting over with a new foster family. But at least I get to leave school each day if kids hurt me; I don't always get that option at bad foster homes.

"Actually, Anna, you guys are going to the same school you were just in."

"You mean I to stay with my same teacher?"

"That's right."

"Oh, that's great! I love my teacher!"

"I'm so glad to hear that. I'm going to come with you and meet your teachers tomorrow."

Parents don't take their kids into class in fifth grade. If Liz walks me into school like I'm a little kid, Marlene will make my life miserable. That can't happen.

"Um. Liz, thank you, but... um... can you just drop me off instead?" I have to say something to make her understand without making things worse. I'm gonna have to... trust her. "I... um... have a mean girl in my class, Marlene, who lived with us in the last foster home."

"She was super mean to Anna," Jenna says. "I didn't like her because she made fun of Anna."

"Would you like to move to a different class so you don't have to see Marlene?" Joe asks.

"No. I really like my teacher." Not to mention I just don't want to have to be moved again. Especially from someone who likes me. I'll just have to deal with Marlene to stay with Mrs. Swing.

"Anna?" Liz grins at me and I'm jealous of her pretty white—and straight—teeth. Mine are awful. There's nothing attractive about buck teeth.

"What does Marlene do to you?" Liz asks.

Where should I even begin? "Um, she's mean. She tries to get other kids to laugh at me."

"Well, that's not nice. But I have an idea. Wanna hear it?"

A foster parent who wants to help me with my life? Of *course* I want to hear it. "Yeah!"

"How about..." She glances at Joe. "...if we get you some cool clothes tonight, and I'll bring in my killer cupcakes in for everyone!"

Ohmygosh. I can't even speak. I'm so happy. My class is crazy about cupcakes—and, this time, Mrs. Swing won't have to bring them in for me! I have a foster mom who will actually do this—for *me*!

"Can you make them for my class, too?" Jenna whispers.

"Oh, I would *never* forget about you, Jenna. We treat everyone the same in this house." She looks at Joe. "Well, I guess it's gonna be a girls' night tonight. I'll take them shopping then swing by the bakery to grab two dozen of the cupcakes we have."

Wait, what? I thought Liz was gonna make them. "What's a bakery?"

"It's my family-owned bakery." Liz stands up. "Let me call your teachers to find out how many kids are in your classes."

Wow. Liz has her own bakery where she has cupcakes! I can't wait to see it!

Joe stands up. He's so huge that if I didn't know he was so nice, I'd seriously be afraid of him. "I've got to head back to work, girls. I work the night shift, which means I'm working while you sleep, and sleeping while you're awake, so if you can try to be quiet when you get home from school, I'd greatly appreciate it. Have fun shopping. Head out to the car and get in; Liz will be right with you. And don't forget to grab your coats because it's cold out there."

Oh, we know cold, all right… At least now, it's gonna be outside and not where we sleep.

Yeah, I think this place is gonna be pretty nice. It's already better than Jane and Roger's. And things just keep getting better when we get to the store. Liz tells us we can pick out whatever we want.

I've never been in a store this size before, and one with all this stuff. I don't know how I'm gonna choose!

"Follow me girls," says Liz. "We'll head over to the department with your sizes."

When we get there, Jenna disappears into the clothes, but me? I don't know what to do. I've never done this before. How do I shop? I don't want to look strange to Liz, so I move clothes around on a rack.

"Anna? Do you know what size you wear?"

I shake my head. Not only do I not know what size I am, I don't even know how old I am.

"Well, you're a small little for a ten-year-old. This is a size eight; it might fit."

Wait. Did she just say that I'm small for a *ten-year-old*? I knew it! I *was* right, and Jane was clueless. Or did Jane know and she was just trying to make me mad?

Liz points to the room. "Head in there and try it on to see if it fits."

"I have to take my clothes off in there?"

"Of course, if you want to try on the shirt."

I do *not* want to take my clothes off in a store, no matter the reason. But I'll pretend to go in there, so Liz doesn't think I'm weird. But I don't like shopping now.

The storeroom has a mirror. I hold my shirt up against me. Yup. It

Just Another Door

looks like it will fit. I do the same with the pants that Liz gave me to try on, though they're size nine. I hold them up to my legs. They'll fit, too. Good, I'm done.

"Wow, Anna, you're fast. Jenna is still in there, trying on all kinds of clothes. Would you like to try on some more?"

"No, thanks." I'm not trying on anything. I'm not going to take my clothes off in this store because you never know who's gonna open the door and walk in.

Finally, Jenna comes out with a huge stack of clothes. "Can I get all of them?" she asks as a few fall off her arms.

"Sure, if you like them."

"I do." Jenna jumps and claps at the same time dropping the clothes in her arms. She giggles as she bends over and picks them up.

Me? I want to get in the car and go back to the house as fast as we can. All kinds of men are walking around those rooms that Liz wanted me to take my clothes off in. That will never happen, even when I'm big.

"Can we leave now Liz? I'm tired." I feel trapped in this store, and I want to get out.

"C'mon, Anna, we only hit one store. I want to shop more." Jenna sounds upset with me.

"You know what, Jenna? Maybe you and I can go shopping at another time. Anna is tired. You've both had a long day."

She's right; I am tired. All the thinking I had to do in that dressing room was exhausting.

But my tiredness goes away when we get to the baker. The big wood sign reads, "Zeta's Bakery."

"What does that name mean Liz?"

She turns around from the front seat. "Zeta refers to the letter "Z "in Greek and in Roman. Since our last name starts with the letter, we thought this would be a great name for the bakery.

"Oh." This foster answers all my questions all the time so far and she doesn't act mad when I ask either.

This place smells like *Heaven*.

And it looks just as pretty too. There are large windows that have a big flower wreath around them, and there are rows and rows of cookies and cakes and breads and cupcakes on shelves behind glass doors. This place smells like flowers and sugar all together.

Liz puts her arm around me. "Anna, do you like this place?"

Dr. Sharon Zaffarese-Dippold

Though I don't like people touching me, I'm okay with Liz doing it because she's nice and lets me make my own choices and asks for my opinion and isn't creepy and doesn't have a creepy husband. She doesn't make me uncomfortable like a lot of other people in my life. Maybe that's why I don't mind… I might even… like it…. "I love this place—it smells *amazing*."

"That makes me happy to hear. I feel the same way." She squeezes my shoulder a little. "Let's get your cupcakes picked out—and don't forget to pick on for you to eat on the way home."

Wow, this woman is *seriously* the best. I've never been able to make this many decisions before and I'm loving it.

There are so many to choose from! I take my time, but the big red-and-green ones that look like Christmas with candy on top of them are the ones I want. "Can I have the ones that go with the Christmas tree colors?"

"Consider it done." Liz looks at the lady behind the counter. "Hey, Michelle. Please box up two dozen of the "After-Christmas" cupcakes."

And just like that, I get what I want. Is this how easy it's supposed to be?

I think I've lived with so many bad families that I don't know what *real* life is supposed to be like. And how sad—and sucky—is *that*!

Jenna picks ones that look like Valentine's Day, all red with white swirls on them. Liz gets the same amount for her class.

I can't *wait* 'til school tomorrow. Marlene better keep her mouth shut if she wants a giant cupcake.

We get home and put the boxes onto the kitchen counter.

"I'm hungry." Jenna says.

She has a point. "We forgot our cupcakes, Liz!" I say. "You know, the ones you said we can have now?"

"Who says I forgot?"

She pulls out a box from behind her back. In it, is a cupcake for each of us.

Jenna and I bang our cupcakes together with a "Cheers!" cracking each other up. We've done more fun stuff in this house than we ever did at Jane and Roger's. It feels good to be happy… but, I'm afraid to like it. Everything changes all the time, and I already know this isn't the family I'm going to stay with.

It's such a shame. I finally have a cool foster mother and no one's gonna let me stay with her. Well, at least tomorrow will be good. Especially 'cause these cupcakes are way bigger than what Marlene brought to class. These will make what she brought in look sick, and, for once, I won't be the weird one. *And* I'll have on my cool new clothes.

Yeah, it's gonna be a good day. Finally, I get to be proud of how I look and am in school.

Mrs. Swing greets me and Liz as soon as I walk into the classroom—actually, she *hugs* me. None of my other teachers has ever done that before.

I'm not sure if I should hug her back, so I just stand there.

"Hello, Anna. I'm so glad you're out of that house and living with Ms. Liz!" She smiles at Liz. "We were best friends in school."

"You… were?" Why didn't Liz tell me this? I told her my teacher's name.

"Yes," Liz says. "We've stayed in touch all of these years. Matter of fact, Mrs. Swing is one of the reasons Joe and I became foster parents."

"Speaking of Joe," Mrs. Swing says, "he *is* coming into class tomorrow to talk about being a police officer, right?"

"Oh, he's definitely going to be here. He's doing it for Anna."

Liz hugs her. "You and Officer Joe are what the foster care system needs." She takes a big breath, then looks at me. "Well, Anna, are you ready to walk in with your treat?"

"I am! I'm super excited about today."

"Here you go, Ms. Anna." Liz hands me two boxes of cupcakes, then wishes me a good day. "Go give everyone a tasty surprise from the best bakery in town. I'll see you at home later."

My head is high as I walk in holding my treat for the class. I can't wait to hand them out.

"Whatcha gonna do, foster kid?"

Of *course,* Marlene has to stand up and act like she's better than me—I expected no less. And this time, I'm gonna show her what I'm going to do.

Chapter 15
A Dream

Marie's voice snaps me out of my thoughts of Marlene. That girl runs through my mind a lot. I spend all day worrying about what she's going to say or do. I can defend myself if I have to, but I don't like the names and teasing. But today it's cupcake day and I'm happy. I'm not going to let her ruin that for me. She'll get her cupcake last, so I don't have to hear how great or better her mother is as I walk around the room, passing them out.

These two big boxes are super heavy. I can barely lift them. With a *whoosh* of movement, Marie runs toward me, sending a chair flying into another desk.

She points at the white boxes in my hands. "Mornin', Anna. What's that?"

"My new foster mother, Liz, baked them in her bakery. She said I can bring some to class this morning."

Marie's mouth hangs open, as if she's expecting something to fly in. "So, you have a new foster mom now? That's sucks."

"Not really. Joe and Liz are nice fosters, and I like staying with them so far. Though it's only been a night, look what they did for me." I lift the boxes.

"I think I like them too." She giggles as she opens the container to see all the cupcakes.

"Yes, they are very nice people. Marie head back to your desk, please."

We both jump. I didn't know Mrs. Swing was standing behind us "Look, class, Anna Snow brought in cupcakes from Zeta's Bakery." Mrs. Swing claps and the rest of the kids join her. "We're all in for a treat this morning. Now, let's get to your seats."

I can't believe kids are clapping, I'm used to them calling me names and laughing at me. My face turns red. I feel embarrassed. This is a new feeling. Getting angry at kids for being mean is easy. This feeling…is weird. I don't like it.

Marlene stands up and points at me. "Of *course,* she has a new foster mother—my parents kicked her and Jenna out because they're scumbags. I was hoping that I'd never see her again. And here she is, still in my class. Yuk."

"Marlene's voice is louder than the applause for the treats I brought in.

Oh, no. Liz's plan won't work after all, because Marlene just ruined it. And now, I'm going to knock her out right in front of everyone. I don't have to worry about the basement anymore. That was one thing protecting her. I step towards Marlene.

"Anna, why don't you start handing out your cupcakes on this side of the room?" She points to the opposite side that Marlene sits. Though Marlene is closer to the middle and in the front row. So, I'll start with the back. Then, out of nowhere, Marie stands on her chair again.

"Your *mother* sucks as a foster parent. She never did anything like this for Anna. Maybe she ought to get a new job because she *sucks* at foster care."

Mrs. Swing looks frozen for a second. Then she talks again. "Marie, please step down from your chair before you fall and take your seat. Anna will pass out the cupcakes. And Marlene, you will be the last one to receive yours this morning. If there are other mean words you'd like to say, you'll not be getting one at all."

Two people are sticking up for me, Marie and Mrs. Swing. I love it here; I really do. It feels good knowing that there are people in this world who like me enough to stick up for me. If I would've jumped that night in the woods, I wouldn't be standing here now. And... I like being here.

"Marlene's in trouble, Marlene's in trouble. She won't be getting a cupcake," a boy sings.

For the first time, Marlene puts her head down—she's not enjoying being the one picked on.

Welcome to my world, Marlene.

"Shut up, retard," she says, the moment not lasting long. "Your parents are poor and live on welfare."

"Enough! Both of you stop!" Mrs. Swing yells. "Go ahead, Anna, and pass out your cupcakes."

Marie's at the back and I start with her.

"Thanks, Anna!" She takes the cupcake with the most icing and wolfs down a huge bite before I get to the next kid.

Everyone's acting great and nice to me, and they're super excited! This feels so good. I've never had kids like me like this at school before. No one is saying anything about my teeth or my clothes. I'm so glad Mrs. Swing doesn't let kids in her class bully other ones—even Marlene, though she deserves it.

And I really wanna smash the cupcake I have for her in her face. But I won't since I'd get in big trouble.

I don't want anything to ruin this moment, so I hand it to her.

"You let the other kids pick out theirs, so I want to pick my own. I don't want your grubby hands on it

"Take it or you don't get any." She can want what she wants all she wants but I'm not gonna make it happen. This is *my* day, not hers.

Marlene rips the cupcake from my hand. "I hope this doesn't kill me."

"You're fine. We ran out of poison," I snarl back.

The kids burst into laughter.

"She ran out of poison—that's funny, Anna!" a kid named Ty, one of the popular kids, yells from the other side of the room.

Ha! The popular kid is laughing at Marlene—and after she worked so hard to hang out with him and his friends. I guess they're not the friends Marlene thought. I mean, *my* friend doesn't laugh at me; she actually yells at the person who does it to me. I'm glad I have Marie rather than the popular kids. Having a *real* friend is better than *saying* you have a bunch of friends... who'll laugh at you in front of other people.

Just Another Door

I bring what's left to my teacher's desk. "Here's one for you, Mrs. Swing." I give her the last cupcake.

"What about you, Anna?" She hands it back to me.

"Nope, I'm good. Liz gave me one last night."

"Well, thank you, Anna." She peels the wrapper back and takes a bite. "Ms. Liz's cupcakes are the best."

Walking back to my desk, I pass a whole bunch of kids grinning, icing all over their teeth. They all thank me.

A girl—who's never said a word to me before—tells me she likes my sneakers. Another girl says my T-shirt is cool. Wow! I've never had people like me like this. I feel—normal. Today, I'm not a foster kid, but another student in the class. I'm *part* of something and no longer the weird outcast.

Thank you, Joe and Liz.

As I sit down, I glance at Marlene. Her hair and face are bright red. She's pissed and I have a feeling that she's gonna do something at recess to make me pay. I'll have to be on my guard. But that might just make today even better.

"Come on, Anna. We're in the hopscotch finals this morning. We need you." Marie grabs my hand and pulls me out the door.

At the starting line, I stare at number seven where I want my rock to land. I wind up and—

I fall backward.

My head's on fire 'cause someone's yanking my hair and it's getting ripped out.

Then I hit the concrete—

And get punched in the face.

Red hair falls in my eyes.

Marlene. Of course. I called it.

I shove her.

She falls off, hitting the hard ground with a *thud*.

I leap up. She's *not* going to get the best of me. I've beaten bigger—and more—kids than stupid Marlene.

"Fight! Fight!" kids scream as they circle around us.

Marlene gets to her feet, holding her hands in front of her face. As if they're going to protect her... ha!

I swing, my fist connecting with her nose.

A sharp *crack* splits the air and blood sprays everywhere.

"You're a total jerk! Look what you did!" she cries like a baby as she tries to catch the blood pouring out of her nose.

"What *I* did? Look at my face." I'm not even sure if there's anything wrong with it, but it hurts like crazy.

"Fight! Fight! Fight!" The kids around us keep screaming.

"What in the world is happening?" A teacher bursts into the circle.

"Anna just decked me for nothing." Blood spurts between Marlene's fingers.

"Let's get you inside to see Nurse Faye." The teacher takes her by the arm.

"What's going on?" Mrs. Swing says as she runs up.

"Marlene pulled Anna's hair, making her fall down," a kid from my class says.

I don't know who he is, but I do know he loved his cupcake. It's paying off now since he's standing up for me.

"Yeah. We all saw it! Marlene sat on top of Anna and punched her in the face," said another student I don't know, but who sits near Marlene. She also liked her cupcake. "I saw the whole thing. Anna didn't do anything to start it."

"Thanks, Stephanie, for the info." Mrs. Swing rests her hand on my shoulder. "Are Stephanie and Bruce being honest about what really happened?"

For once someone—*two* someones—are standing up for me. "Yes, they are. I was about to throw my rock in the game when Marlene pulled my hair and made me fall backward. Then she jumped on me and punched me. When I stood up, she tried to punch me again, but I decked her before she could get another punch off."

Mrs. Swing turns my head with her hand on my chin. "Mmmm. I see that you have a big red spot on your cheek. Come with me so we can get you seen by Nurse Faye and a report taken."

"Am I in trouble?" I don't want to make Liz or Joe mad at me.

"No. It sounds like you were defending yourself."

"Yes, I *was* protecting myself." It's nice to know that I'm not going to get into trouble because of someone starting crap with me. I'm *done* letting people hurt me; I'll fight back if they try.

In the nurse's office, Nurse Faye's working on Marlene's nose. "Have a seat, Anna," the nurse says. "I'll be right with you."

Well, it definitely doesn't sound like I'm going to get into trouble. But then Mr. Jim walks into the office.

Oh, no. Did Mrs. Swing tell him something like she told him before, thinking she was doing the right thing? She said she'd never do that again.

"I've contacted your foster father," Mr. Jim says. "He'll be here shortly."

Am I going to have to kiss this nice home goodbye when I didn't even *do* anything except defend myself? "Is he... um... is he upset?"

Mr. Jim shakes his head. "Concerned, but not mad."

I don't know what the heck that means. What's the difference? Why bother asking, I don't really want to talk with Mr. Jim right now anyway.

"What happened here?" Joe walks into the office just as Nurse Faye is done doing what she can for Marlene's face. "Hey, Anna." He cups my cheek. "It looks like she got you good." He glances at Nurse Faye. "I'm getting tired of the assaults on Anna by that other student. Something needs to be done to stop it."

Principal Jim comes out. "Hello, Officer Joe. I've been hearing the conversation. How are you connected with Ms. Anna Snow?"

"Good day, Principal Jim. We are providing care for Ms. Anna." Their hands meet in a handshake. "You can see why I'm worried about the constant bullying." Joe's voice drops. He's serious.

"We will handle the matter." He looks at me.

"I advise you to manage the situation more effectively." Joe turns to leave.

The nurse pops into the main office. "Hey, Officer Joe, I want to have a look at Anna before you go." Nurse Faye has a sweet voice. "Now, Anna, let me check out that face." She turns my head. "Hmmm. You've got a bruise. It'll be sore for a few days, and turn black-and-blue, but, don't worry, it will heal. Can I feel the back of your head to make sure there is not cuts?"

"Sure." *C'mon Anna, this will only take a second.* The idea of someone running their hands through my hair makes my whole-body quiver. I hate that feeling just like I hate people brushing my hair. I think it's because Mother, my first foster, would pull my hair hard to get the knots.

"Looks like you smacked the back of your head when you fell, too."

She pokes around a little—it hurts when she does that—then she says, "Joe, keep an eye on her so she doesn't fall asleep for the next couple of hours."

"Will do. Come on, Anna. Let's get you home." Joe nudges me toward the door, then shakes Mr. Jim's hand. "Take care of this for me, Jim, okay?"

Principal Jim nods.

Just as Joe opens the back door of the cop car for me, Marlene and Jane show up on the sidewalk.

"Hello, Anna." Her voice all crackly like she just got done smoking.

I'm not saying anything to this woman. I told her what her nasty husband was doing and she did nothing about it except get rid of us. She'll never see what her sweet Marlene does wrong if she won't admit what Roger was capable of.

Marlene walks right up to me and puts her fist in the air.

Joe steps between us, facing Marlene. "And what do you think you're doing, young lady?"

"Please don't talk to my daughter, officer," Jane snaps.

"If your daughter continues to harass and bully Anna, I'll be talking to her *and* you… when I press charges." Joe puts his arm around me. "Let's go, Anna."

I hop into the back of the cop car. He just stuck up for me and said that he would press charges.

"Are you okay, kiddo? I'm sure it wasn't easy to come face-to-face with either of them."

He's right about that; I can't stand 'em. But I don't want him to worry about me because I can take care of myself. Didn't I just prove it? "I'm good." I don't want to sound dumb asking him what charges mean. Whatever it is, Jane didn't like it because she walked away. That's all I need to know.

"All right, then. But if you need to talk, let me know." He smiles in his rearview mirror. Mrs. Alex always does this with me, too, but I like it better from Joe because he's not taking me some place I don't want to go like Mrs. Alex always does. Well, except this last time when she brought me to Joe's house. Then, I'd been *more* than happy to get in her ugly green monster car.

As we pull into the driveway, I see that stupid awful car again. Oh no. "Am I leaving now, Joe?"

"Not that I'm aware of, and I'm sure we'd know if that was happening." He turns off the engine. "Let's get inside so we can find out together."

Just Another Door

I follow him into the house even though I really don't wanna. I don't want to leave these nice people. I've only been here one day; how could Mrs. Alex have found another home already? Can't I get a break? My head feels heavy like it's broken and the only thing I can do is look at the floor. Why does she take all the nice families away from me? I didn't do anything. Does she want me to be sad? Does she want people to hurt me? I don't get it.

"Hello, Mrs. Alex," Joe says. "What a nice surprise."

No, it's not a nice surprise at all. Why do people say that? Does he mean it or is he doing a fake nice?

"Anna," Liz says, "take a seat with Jenna. We had to pick her up early today so you both can be here at the same time."

This is bad. I just know it.

Lifting my head so I can see where I'm going, I do as she says. Are they moving both of us now? We couldn't even finish out the school day.

Mrs. Alex clears her throat. "I want to discuss your placement with the Zells with both of you."

Oh no! I was right. She *did* find us a foster home, and we hafta leave. My hands get all wet and my chest starts hurting like it always does when bad things happen. *Just* when I thought I could stay in a nice home with nice people—even for a short time—it gets ripped out from under me. I hate my life.

"Girls, the Zells have requested to become your foster parents, and I wanted to be—"

"Yay!!!" Jenna and I jump up and hug each other.

I can't believe what I'm hearing! I get to stay! *We* get to stay! This really is the Best. Day. Ever. First cupcakes, then the kids liking me—and Marlene getting her face all bloody—Joe standing up for me and now this! I don't think I've ever been this happy!

"I guess this means the two of you are okay with this plan?" Mrs. Alex asks.

Finally, we have a say. *Finally*, I get to decide what I want. About time. "Yes, Mrs. Alex! I want to stay here! Yes! Yes! Yes!" I can't say *yes* enough times!

"Well, it sounds like I'm not needed anymore." Mrs. Alex stands up. "If you two need anything," she says to Joe and Liz, "don't hesitate to reach out to me."

"We're good. Thank you, Mrs. Alex. Joe shakes her hand.

Jenna runs over to Liz after Mrs. Alex leaves and wraps her arms around her. "Can I call you Mom now?"

That didn't take long; Jenna likes to call the foster Mom and Dad. Not me—though this home may make me change my mind.

"You are welcome to call me whatever you like Jenna." Liz puts her hand over her heart. "I'm honored to have you call me Mom."

Jenna jumps up and hugs her. I wish I was ready to call her mom because Liz acts happy about it. But, I just can't yet.

To celebrate this happy occasion as a family, we decided to go out and get some ice cream. Joe grabs his jacket. "I love to say that…" He smiles at us both. "Family. I will protect both of you. That's what a dad does."

My heart sinks. Daddy said he protected me by sending me away. He. Protected me. Tears find their way to my eye lashes fast. This is the first time since him, that someone wanted to be my daddy. I'm happy and sad at the same time. I hope that I can let Joe be my daddy, because he would be a great one. But, that's what I thought about Sue too and look at what she did to me. She hurt me with secret girl time. I have to wait and see who these people really are.

We all pile in the car. Joe sings along to some rock music while Liz tells him to turn it down. This is definitely not country music like I used to listen to with daddy.

Mint chocolate chip, here I come.

"We're excited to have you both with us. It just all seemed like a good fit for us all." Joe wipes at his face.

Is he crying? That's what people do when they cry. I can't see because he turned his head the other way.

"I agree, Joe." I slurp up a chip.

"Me, too." Jenna likes chocolate.

"How are you two feeling?" Liz asks.

"I'm happy, Mom. You guys are the best."

She's right. They totally rock. I'm happy to be staying here. But I'm really afraid to. Can all of this be real? What I know about fosters, they change after a while. People aren't always what they seem. I have to keep my eyes open and watch them. Any little thing can tell me that they're changing. When that happens, I'll need to look for a hiding place fast.

The ride home is quiet—but a good quiet, not a scary one. My body likes these people—my mind isn't racing with all kinds of scary thoughts and I'm not shaking, and my chest stopped hurting when Mrs. Alex told us the good news. Plus, so *far*, I don't have to worry about finding a hiding place for us.

"Before we get out of the car, we have another surprise for you both in the house. But we have to let Joe go in first."

"I'll flip the porch light on when I'm ready," Joe says, "then you can come in."

"Okay, Dad." Jenna answers before anyone else can. She leans close to me, "Can you believe it, Anna? We can be real sisters, and we don't have to sleep in the basement or worry about Roger anymore."

Real sisters? I won't be alone anymore. Snowstorm can be together forever. Or can we. What happens if they take Jenna away from me like they did Curtis? I can't go through that again. If they can take my real brother from me, Mrs. Alex can definitely take Jenna who is just my foster sister. And maybe, Joe and Liz will decide they want her to leave just like Jessica and her husband did with Curtis. Then, I'm all alone again. My heart races fast as I think about all the bad things that can happen.

"Anna? Did you hear me?"

"Yes, I did. I'm happy about that to." I grab her hand and squeeze. "We are real sisters." It seems like we're waiting forever.

The porch light finally flashes. "Time to go in, girls."

Jenna jumps out of the car at the same time Liz does. "I'll race you, Jenna screams."

She reaches the door first. "C'mon, slow pokes!"

"Follow me!" Liz giggles like one of us as she leads us into the house.

So far, I see nothing. We walk up the stairs to the dining room.

Nothing.

Then we move downstairs to the living room.

Nothing.

"Are you two ready?" Liz has her hand on a closet door.

"Is the surprise in there?" I ask.

"Yes, we're ready." Jenna yells.

"It is!" Liz flings open the door.

Forget a closet, it's a room! And a huge, sparkly Christmas tree is in there.

"Merry Christmas, you two!" Joe says as he sits next to a bunch of presents.

Liz grabs our hands and leads us to the tree. "We noticed that you didn't bring any toys with you, and since Christmas was just last week, we thought we'd celebrate it with you again."

"This is amazing!" Jenna screams louder than I've ever heard her.

She's right—I can't believe this is actually happening. Is this family for real?

"Take a seat, girls." Joe' puts on a Santa hat, then picks up a gift. "Jenna, this is for you."

She tears off the wrapping paper of a blonde, skinny doll. "Thank you. I like it."

"Anna, this is for you." Joe hands me a small box.

Slowly, I open it… and pull out a small dress.

This isn't going to fit me. Plus, I forgot to tell Liz I don't like to wear dresses anymore.

"I thought maybe you'd like some clothes for Raggedy. I didn't see that you had anything else for her to wear."

Oooooh… It's not for me. I never thought about Raggedy needing new clothes.

This is really nice of Liz.

"Jenna, this is for you." Joe hands her an enormous box.

She tears through the paper even faster than on her doll and starts jumping up and down. "You got me a dollhouse?! Thank you!"

Joe hands me a medium-sized box. It feels heavy. I feel numb right now. These people don't even know us and they're giving us a Christmas—and with toys we like, not stupid *socks*.

I unwrap it slowly because I can't seem to get my fingers to work. This is all so much.

It's an… an Easy Bake Oven. Just like what Marlene got for Christmas. Now I have one. I really don't know what to say. I've never had anyone think of me like this before. Not even Daddy. We didn't even celebrate Christmas at that house.

And I'd thought I was happy there. That's the… crazy? Funny? Scary? Part of my whole life. I hadn't known what I was missing. Now… I do. Now I know there are bad people in this world and people who don't care about foster kids, but the Zells… They actually do.

Jenna and I are really lucky to have ended up here. I hope we get to be a family for a long long time.

"I'll help you set it up if you like." Liz points to the picture on the box. "Look at all the things you can make."

I want to cry because I'm so happy. But I won't. Not if I can help it.

Just Another Door

Happy tears are still tears and no one can see me cry.

Even when I'm happy.

Because... I'm also afraid. Are they being nice to us because they want something from us? Does Liz want girl time? Does Joe want to give us a bath? Why are they so nice?

I hate that I can't just trust that they're nice to be nice. But the Sues and Mrs. Dorseys and Dereks of my world have taught me that many people always want something more.

We get about ten presents each. Mine are the clothes for Raggedy, the oven, a Lite-Brite, more coloring books and story books than I've ever had, crayons, and some more clothes.

Jenna's got a bunch of skinny dolls with pretty outfits to change them into, some reading books, her own coloring books, a Lite-Brite of her own (so we don't hafta share!), and more clothes as well.

And I'd thought last Christmas with Raggedy as my gift was the best Christmas.

Well, I do still love Raggedy. She's my best friend... next to Teddy, I guess. Though, I guess I can call Jenna my best friend?

And she's my sister.

I don't want today to ever end.

We sit around the tree as a family, Jenna and I playing with our Lite-Brites. Joe's helping Jenna and Liz is helping me.

"Thank you, Joe and Liz. This was really nice. We didn't get anything at Jane's house except for socks."

"I'm sorry, girls. Sometimes, people have a hard time making good choices for others. But I'm glad you like your gifts."

"Um, Liz?"

"Yes, Anna,"

"We didn't get you anything." This makes me sad. They did so much for us already.

Liz hugs me.

My body goes still like a board... but it doesn't stop Liz from squeezing me. I don't want to like her till I know she won't be like Sue. Maybe she's hugging me now and later might want me to do something else to her. I don't want to hug her back but I do at the same time. Please don't be like Sue Liz, please. She let's go.

"You and Jenna are the only gifts we need." She and Joe make goo-goo eyes at each other.

"Yes, we are." Jenna laughs.

I want to be happy. I want to make myself laugh with all of them, But… I'm afraid this isn't real. There's just no way this can be my life right now. Something will happen to mess it up. I just know it.

I slide away from Liz so she's not touching me.

"Are you okay, Anna?"

"Yeah. I'm just tired. Can I go to bed now?"

"Sure, you can, kiddo," Joe says. "Maybe it's a good time for all of us to get going. It's been a long day."

Something will happen to mess this up. I just know it.

A fluffy blanket wraps around my neck perfectly as I get comfortable in bed. The sheets smell so clean. Completely different than my first foster home where our mattress had yellow stuff coming out of it and the only thing I had was a sheet. I appreciate the blankets on my bed. You never know what each foster home will give you.

Jenna is asleep already and I can hear her talking to herself. Then she screams.

"Stop it! Leave me alone. It hurts! It hur…"

I jump off the bed and sit on the edge of my sister's just when Liz and Joe comes barreling into the room.

"What's wrong Anna?"

"It wasn't me. It's Jenna. I think she's having nightmare."

"Can I sit with you?"

"Jenna wake up." Liz rubs her back. "Wake up sweet girl." Liz sounds like she really cares about her. Joe stands over both of us not saying a word.

Jenna's eye's flicker open. "What? What are you all doing on my bed?"

"You were having a nightmare."

Liz lets me talk. She just sits and watches me. It's nice she's letting me help.

"I'm okay Anna. I don't remember my dream. But I'm tired and I want to go to sleep now."

Jenna rolls over like none of us is here.

Jane places her hand on my leg. I pull it away. She looks at me for a second.

"Thank you, Anna, for helping your sister. She's lucky to have you."

I'm the lucky one. I know what it's like to be all alone.

"How about you get up in bed so you can get some sleep." Liz stands heads to the door to stand next to Joe. They wait as I climb back in my bed,

"Good night, Kiddo." Joe switches the light off and closes the door.

Boy is this different than Jane's cold, dark basement. My worlds are so different.

Now, I have a family—Jenna, me, Liz and Joe. I couldn't have picked a better one. So why am I so afraid?

"Jesus. Thank you for this family. You gave me a good one. Now I have a sister, too. Thank you. But why am I afraid? I feel like something's going to happen to take them away from me. Please help me not to be afraid. Goodnight, Jesus."

***

We've been living with Zells for a week and they're still just as nice as they were when we got here. School's been all right. Ever since Joe threatened Jane and Marlene, Marlene's been ignoring me except for the occasional death stare across the classroom. I like not worrying at school all the time. It makes it easier to learn my spelling words.

A knock on the door makes Jenna and me jump. "Good morning, girls." Foster Liz says, sounding like she's in the room with Jenna and I rather than on the other side of the door. "Breakfast is on the table. Can I open the door?"

"Sure," we both say.

Foster Liz never walks into our room without knocking, and neither does Joe. I like this a lot because I don't hafta worry that someone will come in when I'm getting dressed.

"Jenna, can you head downstairs? I'd like to talk with Anna alone. Please close the door on your way out."

Why does Liz want to talk to me alone? I'm totally shaking.

"Okay." Jenna grabs my hand for a quick squeeze before she leaves. She knows this isn't usual around here. Our fosters do not talk with one and send the other one away. Liz and Joe usually talk with both of us together.

This must be serious.

Liz grabs my hand. "I received a phone call from Mrs. Alex this morning. Your birth mother, Norma, would like you to come live with

Dr. Sharon Zaffarese-Dippold

her."

Time stops; everything around me freezes, nothingness replaces all the sounds around me, as if I just went inside a bubble. Every body part is paralyzed. My legs. My arms. My mouth. My heart.

I'm no longer an unwanted kid. My mother wants me.

About the Author

Dr. Sharon Zaffarese-Dippold's writing comes from her own lived experiences as a child who experienced multiple foster care and family placement moves, and involved all forms of abuse and trauma.

Dr. Dippold attended approximately ten or more schools during her formative years as she moved from place to place. In spite of that, she earned a Bachelor in Social Work, a Masters in Social Work, and earned her PhD in Human Services from Capella University, with a concentration in Human Behavior/Counseling Studies.

Her doctoral dissertation was published in 2016, *The Lived Experience Of Former Foster Children Who Had to Move Their Belongings In Garbage Bags*. A public speaker and trainer on foster care topics related to her story, her experience with bullying led her to create "INAM-It's Not About Me," an anti-bullying program she presents in school systems to deflect the impact of being bullied on children.

Dr. Zaffarese-Dippold lives in Saint Mary's, Pennsylvania, with her husband, where she enjoys spending time with her children and grandchildren.

For motivational speaking, book signings, or training events, please contact Dr.Dippold@gmail.com or ZeeTPublishing@gmail.com.

JUST another HOME

The Final Book in the
Garbage Bag Life Series.

Projected Release Date 9/2026

DR SHARON ZAFFARESE-DIPPOLD

Printed in Dunstable, United Kingdom